Linda Murray

Michelangelo

161 illustrations, 20 in color

Thames & Hudson world of art

For Harvey

Published in the United States of America in 1985 by Thames & Hudson Inc., 500 Fifth Avenue, New York, New York 10110

thamesandhudsonusa.com

Reprinted 2000

Library of Congress Catalog Card Number 88-50155
ISBN 0-500-20174-9

Printed and bound in Singapore by C.S. Graphics

Contents

Acknowledgments

Debts of gratitude are always a pleasure to pay, and I am grateful to many friends for their help. Professor L. D. Ettlinger discussed many of the knottier problems with me (and is in no way to blame for my errors of omission or commission, for which I alone am responsible). He also allowed me to read in manuscript his definitive article, 'The Liturgical Function of Michelangelo's Medici Chapel', published in the December 1978 issue of the *Mitteilungen des Kunsthistorischen Institutes in Florenz*. Dr Dal Poggetto took me on a visit to the crypt of the Medici Chapel, and gave me a fascinating survey of his remarkable discoveries there, which he is to publish in a forthcoming book. Mr George Bull has allowed me to use his translations of Vasari's Life of Michelangelo and of Aretino's letter to Michelangelo. The discussion of problems with Professor Roberto Salvini has always been rewarding. I am deeply indebted to my husband for many illuminating comments in front of Michelangelo's works, and also for reading the typescript. Last, and by no means least, my grateful thanks are due to Mrs Rose Walton for her skill and patience in reducing my messy manuscript to perfect order and legibility.

Introduction

Michelangelo was born on 6 March 1475, and died on 18 February 1564 – a lifetime of nearly ninety years.

These ninety years saw changes – political, economic, social, religious – as great, as fundamental, as all-pervasive, as those experienced within a comparable span of time in our own period. Michelangelo was born into a world where small states played at petty power politics, snatching at bits of each other's territories – a town here, a port or a tract of farmland there. It was a world where a strategic castle or a useful access to the sea was deemed to warrant the burden of employing rapacious mercenaries to do the actual conquering, which rarely involved any real fighting, since the art of mercenary generalship lay in so managing a campaign that the enemy conceded defeat as a result of skilful tactical moves, through the display of strength, not by the force of arms.

Economically, the small states depended upon an industrious peasantry, barely free of actual serfdom, totally powerless politically, frequently ravaged by the depredations of armed bands of either employed or – far worse – unemployed mercenaries, but on the whole oppressed more by taxation on its produce than by impediments to production. Socially, the strata of society were fixed and it was very difficult to move from one level to another, except through the Church. There, the constant demand for intelligent and capable administrators, for experts in canon law, for Latinists able to conduct the correspondence of prelates, ensured that for an intelligent boy there was a way out of poverty, off the land, or out of the ranks of urban labourers, via the religious life. Clerical preferment offered the poorest boy – as for instance the peasant boy who became Sixtus IV – the chance to rise to the highest office in the Western world, the throne of St Peter, provided that he possessed ability, strength of character, and an element of luck.

In the 1470s Rome, if not an unchallenged power, was at least one of immense strength and prestige. The settlement in 1417 of the disastrous Schism, and the elimination through the election of Martin V of rival claimants to the papal throne, were followed by the return of the papacy to Italy and the end of the seventy-year exile in Avignon. However much friction might be generated in the endemic struggle between Church and State for local political control, the desire of the majority of the rulers of

Western Europe was still for one set of beliefs and one church for all Christendom.

While there was not always peace and plenty in Italy, reasonable stability was maintained by the elaborate cross-checks which its division into many small states provided. There was a nominal fealty to a German overlordship centred on the Holy Roman Empire, but this troubled few and was a social rather than a political force. The Church held the ultimate power, either through personal excommunication or through general interdict, so that though the balance of power was always precarious it rarely degenerated into outright conflict.

By the time Michelangelo died, all this was changed. Italy had been repeatedly overrun by foreign armies, bent on conquest, loot and power, from the time of the first French invasion in 1494, until the final defeat of Francis I in 1525.

It was the Spaniards who emerged as the eventual controllers of the country. All the smaller states became either subservient to them by policy, allied to them by marriage, or dominated by their military strength – all with the exception of Venice, which managed, by a combination of diplomatic skill and economic strength, to survive as the one state in the peninsula to retain its independence and most of its mainland territories.

Two other things resulted from the Spanish hegemony besides the physical presence of the conqueror and the shadow that fell from his overlordship on the smaller states. One was economic stagnation, and a rise in the cost of living, amounting during the ninety-odd years of Michelangelo's lifetime to about 60 per cent in steady steps, interspersed with frequent wild fluctuations of up to 250 per cent when famine resulting from war, plague or unseasonable weather caused the loss of harvests. The other was a strengthening of social rigidity, the division of society into a nobility possessing great wealth and power, and a poor and totally disenfranchised labouring class. What middle class existed was small and powerless, and imbued with a sense of its precariousness and vulnerability; never able to compete with the great ones of the earth, it was all too conscious of how small a step there was between itself and the nameless poor. Outside the Church, which still remained the chief ladder of social promotion, a few men rose by force of intellect and ability. They were chiefly poets and artists, and the status of the artist changed totally from the superior artisan class of even so able a man as Verrocchio or Ghirlandaio, through the recognition of superior genius first accorded to Leonardo da Vinci, and enjoyed and reinforced by Raphael and Michelangelo.

The greatest changes of all took place in the religious field. Voices had been raised against the Church, at first sporadically and then with increasing persistence. The Waldensians in Savoy and Piedmont who filtered covertly from the late thirteenth century onwards over France and northern Italy despite unremitting persecution were followed by Wyclif and the Lollards in England in the late fourteenth century and by John Hus in Bohemia from the end of the fourteenth century. After Hus was burnt in 1415, there came a long and bitter civil war which lasted until the mid-1460s, and the Hussite cause also became a rallying-point for the Waldensians. When Luther appeared in the early sixteenth century he was the culmination of a long, slow surge against Rome which had been building up over at least two centuries. In the ensuing storm, the Universal Church virtually disappeared, and Christendom was split up into dissident groups, most of which were antagonistic to one another. Half of Germany, half the Netherlands, large parts of France, all Scandinavia, and eventually England and Scotland, broke with Rome. The mental shock of rejection, the physical shock of invasion and devastation by the armies of Spain, a power outwardly professing union with Rome, but prepared to use Lutheran soldiery in an attack on Rome itself to achieve its political aims, provoked in Italy a failure of heart and courage, a deep pessimism, made the blacker by the realization that what had happened was largely the fault of the Church itself. Opulence, corruption, pluralism, nepotism, pastoral inadequacy, rejection of any argument which might involve a compromise with entrenched opinions, blind confidence in the power to enforce obedience, unwillingness to reform, and refusal to hold a Council except on terms which the papacy could itself dictate and control – all these factors contributed to the gloom which afflicted pious men and women during the long period after the Sack of Rome in 1527. The upsurge of renewed confidence did not really come until after Michelangelo was dead. The period of the Counter Reformation was one of bitter reappraisal of the changed circumstances in the life of the Church, and the vicissitudes suffered by the Council of Trent did not encourage any serious thinker to expect quick or effective remedies.

The Council, reluctantly agreed to by Paul III, should have met in 1537, but was delayed until December 1545. Its sessions were frequently interrupted by political tensions, and once by plague, but were held in 1545–47, 1551–52 and 1562–63. While the greater part of its business was concentrated upon theological matters, the last session in December 1563, two months before Michelangelo's death, was particularly important since the role of images in churches was then defined, and therefore the whole question of religious art – so vehemently condemned and so widely destroyed by Protestant zealots – was regulated. The most important rulings concerned orthodoxy, the use of the nude, and decorum. All religious images destined for churches had to be seen and authorized by the bishop of the diocese, to ensure that they conformed to the Church's teaching. The nude was virtually proscribed in religious art, except for such scenes as the Crucifixion and the Lamentation, and so far did this puritanical attitude go that in 1559, during Michelangelo's lifetime, Paul IV employed Daniele da Volterra to paint loincloths on the nudes in the *Last Judgment* in the Sistine Chapel (hence his nickname of 'the breeches-maker'), and Pius V in 1566 ordered a further 'robing' to be done by Girolamo da Fano which mutilated many of the finest figures. It was only with difficulty that Clement VIII, pope from 1592 to 1605, was persuaded by petitions from the Accademia di S. Luca, the artists' academy, to desist from his project of destroying the whole fresco. The nude was deemed acceptable only in mythologies, since to ban it there would be to repudiate all antique art; though Pius V, alarmed at the number of nude mythological figures lovingly collected by his predecessors, gave many of them away and closed the Vatican galleries so that those which remained should no longer be seen in the papal palace.

Under the ruling of decorum, or lack of it, any incident not mentioned in the Bible, or deducible from it, was banned. There were to be no more charming Madonnas spooning soup into the Christ Child's mouth, no more anguished mothers fainting at the foot of the Cross: no Gospel recorded the first, and John says firmly, 'She stood.' There were to be no more fanciful scenes from the Apocryphal Gospels, no more tales of wonder from the Golden Legend: the new iconography enjoined the depiction of the visions and ecstasies of the saints, or of cruel martyrdoms, to encourage missionaries in their fervour.

Even the changed position of the artist brought with it difficulties which barely counterbalanced the advantages of his new status. Once, he had been a member of a team, a workshop, trained by apprenticeship in the methods of his master. He was a craftsman, attentive to the wishes of his patron, following the conventions of his day and able perhaps to create new ones, but if all else failed still craftsman enough to earn a livelihood in another more successful man's shop. The new status which the fame of Leonardo, Raphael and Michelangelo – above all of Michelangelo – enabled him to aspire to was one he could only achieve if he were endowed with exceptional genius. Instead of having to be subservient to the wishes of his client, the artist of genius was now courted and his works sought after because they came from his hand. Great workshop mastery was now less important than the possession of individual genius, and the degree of expression of personal taste, imagination, creativeness, divides artists into two markedly distinct groups: the recognized great masters, and the rest – the practitioners.

The literary aspects of art also began to intrude upon the scene. Ghiberti wrote his *Commentaries* (datable from just before his death in 1455) as a record of his own achievements, and also as the first coherent history of modern art. When Vasari began to write his epoch-making work, the *Lives of the Painters, Sculptors, and Architects* . . . , first published in 1550, his aim was quite different. His purpose was to set out, by a blend of theoretical discussion and biographies, the immeasurable superiority of Florence as a creative centre and of Tuscans as masters of the arts. His first edition ended with a Life of Michelangelo, the only living artist accorded such an honour in his book. He took great pains in the composition of his work and in the research he did for it, and if later scholarship has proved him sometimes wrong in his record, this does not invalidate his importance, since he is so often the only authority and is, in any case, four hundred years nearer the events he is writing about than modern historians. As the starting words of an argument or an investigation, 'Vasari says . . .' remains still the most vivid and valuable testimony to his labours, without which Western art history would in many instances be like a building without a cornerstone. He published a revised and enlarged edition in 1568, four years after Michelangelo's death, which contained the biographies of other living artists, so that Michelangelo's original position in the work was subtly changed, and he took the opportunity to put the record straight by publishing the documents that contradicted statements made by Ascanio Condivi, in his *Life of Michelangelo*, published in 1553, which was a biography virtually dictated by its subject. It is clear from Condivi's *Life* that Michelangelo had come to believe in his own legend. Moreover, during the interval between Vasari's first edition and Michelangelo's death in 1564, Vasari had become a devoted friend, so that his later Life is an admirable biography and appraisal of his subject's work in all the fields in which he laboured.

Vasari's 1568 Life, Condivi's *Life*, and Michelangelo's own letters, form the basis for any study of the artist and his works, and hence are the foundation of this, as of all other, books written about him.

2 Masaccio *The Tribute Money* (detail) 1425/26

3 Michelangelo Drawing after Masaccio's *Tribute Money* *c.* 1489/90

4 Michelangelo Drawing after Giotto *c.* 1489/90

5 Michelangelo Drawing after a lost Masaccio

CHAPTER ONE

Early Works

Michelangelo was the second son of Lodovico Buonarroti, who at the time the boy was born, on 6 March 1475, was near the end of his term of office as *podestà*, or mayor, of Caprese, a small town some thirty miles north of Arezzo. When he was barely a month old the family returned to Florence, to live near Sta Croce in a house which represented a large part of their wealth, and which they shared with Lodovico's mother, and with his brother and his brother's wife. They had all come down in the world from a more prosperous past: Lodovico had no employment after his return to Florence, and before his wife died in 1481 three more sons were born to them. Michelangelo was put out to a wet-nurse in Settignano who was the wife and daughter of stonemasons, and in later life he used to joke that he had imbibed his love of sculpture with her milk. Despite his claims that he evaded his formal schooling, being punished for drawing instead of learning his grammar – the usual legends of an artist's childhood – the literary ability displayed in his letters and poems proves the contrary.

It is clear, however, that there was family opposition to his desire to become an artist, and only reluctantly did Lodovico finally apprentice him to Ghirlandaio, the most successful painter in Florence, a man with a solid reputation and a large workshop. The indenture was signed on 1 April 1488, when Michelangelo was just thirteen. In later life he denied that he had received any formal training in the arts because he wished to encourage the belief that his genius was God-given, and owed nothing to any teacher. Vasari, in his 1550 Life, mentioned this apprenticeship; Condivi, in the 1553 *Life*, expressly denied it; Vasari, in his 1568 Life, published the document which vindicated his accuracy. It must have been during Michelangelo's short stay in the Ghirlandaio workshop that he learned the technique of fresco-painting, for his master was a notable executant in fresco and had just received the commission for the series of the Lives of the Virgin and St John the Baptist in the choir of Sta Maria Novella. During this period also he made the early drawings which show his superlative draughtsmanship well developed: the figure of St Peter after Masaccio's fresco of the *Tribute Money* *3, 2* in the Brancacci Chapel, two figures after Giotto from one of the frescoes in *4* Sta Croce, and a superb group of three men, probably after a lost Masaccio in *5*

6 Domenico Ghirlandaio *Baptism of Christ* (detail) 1485–90

7 (*right*) Domenico Ghirlandaio *Presentation of the Virgin* (detail) 1485–90

the Carmine. All showed his mastery of the difficult drawing technique of cross-hatching, as it is by the density of the hatching that he models his forms, and not by any calligraphic use of line. Already, they are sculptor's drawings.

Michelangelo's first steps in his career have long been a problem. The frescoes in the choir of Sta Maria Novella were commissioned by Giovanni Tornabuoni in September 1485, and the contract stipulated that they should be begun in May 1486; they were finished in May 1490. Attempts have been made to identify parts of the choir as by the young Michelangelo, chiefly where a figure by its mass or gravity of treatment departs from the discursive narrative charm of Ghirlandaio's own style, and approaches more closely to the solidity and simplicity of Masaccio's figures in the Brancacci Chapel.

Various suggestions have been made: the bulky draped men on the left in the *Assumption*; the kneeling neophyte in the *Baptism* and the severe draped men behind him; and perhaps to these might be added the nude boy sitting

6

on the steps in the *Presentation of the Virgin* and the two men standing in front of him. The *Assumption* figures may be dismissed at once. Frescoes are painted from the top downwards, and these figures are in the topmost register and would presumably have been executed before Michelangelo's apprenticeship began. The figure on the steps is in the third register from the top of the left wall; the neophyte and his companions in the second register on the right wall. It is not known which wall was started first, but the inscription with the dedication and date is on the right wall, and the width of the choir – some 45 ft (13·7 m) – and the only good source of light from the large triple window (which was not glazed until 1491) make it unlikely that the whole choir was filled with scaffolding at the same time. It is, therefore, not impossible for the groups in the *Presentation* and the *Baptism* to be the young Michelangelo's work, particularly as his deed of apprenticeship specified not only that he should learn, but also that he should paint.

7

If these conjectures are valid, then it would indicate that the young

Michelangelo was developing in a diametrically different manner from the febrile agitated style current in Florence in the last two decades of the Quattrocento – as evidenced in Filippino and Botticelli – and was turning towards a revival of the massive manner of Giotto and Masaccio, and perhaps also towards the greater vigour of Signorelli.

As well as his collection of antique cameos and gems, Lorenzo de' Medici owned a collection of fragments of antique sculpture which he kept in a garden near the monastery of S. Marco. There he employed the ageing Bertoldo, who had been one of Donatello's assistants, to look after them, and while the story told by Vasari that this was a kind of art school which became a forcing-ground for the young talent of the day is now discredited, it appears that a few young men of ability were allowed to study the fragments kept there. Michelangelo's companions included Granacci, the painter to whom he owed his introduction to Ghirlandaio's workshop; Torrigiano, who later came to England to make the tombs of Henry VII and Elizabeth of York in Westminster Abbey, and who described graphically to a disgusted Cellini how he was so enraged by Michelangelo's teasing when they were both drawing in the Brancacci Chapel that he struck him with his clenched fist and broke his nose; Rustici, who came from Verrocchio's studio and later worked with Leonardo, before going to France to do decorative sculpture for Francis I at Fontainebleau; and Baccio da Montelupo, another sculptor

8 DONATELLO *Feast of Herod c.* 1433/35

9 DONATELLO *Madonna and Child*
c. 1425/28

10 MICHELANGELO *Madonna of the Steps*
c. 1491/92

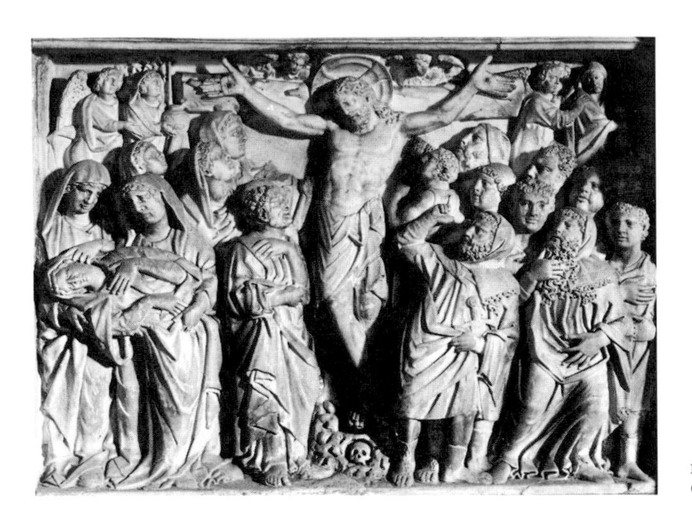

11 NICOLA PISANO
Crucifixion 1260

who became the father of one of Michelangelo's later assistants, Raffaello da Montelupo. The young Michelangelo seems to have impressed Lorenzo since, as both Condivi and Vasari record, he took him into his household and brought him up with his own sons, so that Michelangelo had the advantage for at least two years of surroundings which included the humanist Poliziano, tutor to Lorenzo's children. The foundations of his Neoplatonic and classical interests were laid here, under the influence of Poliziano and other celebrated humanists who visited the Medicean court: Marsilio Ficino, translator of Plato and source of the Platonic inspiration in Michelangelo's later work; Cristoforo Landino, commentator on Virgil and Dante, and another link in the Neoplatonic chain of thought; Pico della Mirandola, humanist, profound scholar of Plato and Aristotle, and the man who attempted to reconcile the Bible with Platonic philosophy. How much contact Michelangelo actually had, how much he later exaggerated his

12 BERTOLDO DI GIOVANNI *Battle of Horsemen c.* 1475

13 MICHELANGELO *Battle of the Centaurs* 1491/92

intimacy with these philosopher-luminaries of the Medicean circle, will never be known, but their influence on a boy in his mid to late teens was so long lasting that it must have been profound at the time. In a very positive way it influenced the rest of his life and the course of his art and thought.

Condivi says that after Michelangelo went to the garden at S. Marco he did not return to Ghirlandaio's workshop, and if it is assumed that he spent about two years in the garden and the Medici household, then the further conjecture that he left Ghirlandaio after the termination of the Sta Maria Novella choir in 1490 also implies that his time in the painter's workshop was short, though sufficient to have given him a good grounding in fresco- and also in easel-painting, since Ghirlandaio was skilled in tempera.

The works attributed to these years are the *Madonna of the Steps* and the *Battle of the Centaurs*. The first is a small, dark yellowish, marble relief showing the Virgin enveloped in fluid draperies with the Christ Child turning His back and burying His head against His mother's breast. Its defects are those of obvious inexperience: the arm of the boy reaching up

10

the balustrade, and the Virgin's right foot curled round her left heel, are clumsy and imperfectly understood. It is also a *tour de force* in that the technique is that of the very low carving often used by Donatello. Vasari remarks that Michelangelo made the relief in emulation of Donatello, which is probably true, since it exploits the same technique as Donatello's *Pazzi Madonna* (Berlin, Staatliche Museen) or the even closer treatment of the
9 theme in his relief now in the Boston Museum. The strange motive of the staircase with the child leaning over it also appears in Donatello's low relief
8 of the *Feast of Herod*, with the interesting possibility (unfortunately no more, since the early history of these reliefs is obscure) that both may have been in the Medici collection, since the inventory made after Lorenzo's death describes two marble reliefs by Donatello which can be interpreted as being these two: one was a *Madonna and Child*, and the other a relief with a lot of perspective in it, figuring a St John. It may be assumed that a young man learning to carve and in daily contact with one of Donatello's chief assistants would have his mind very naturally directed to the earlier master.

13 The *Battle* relief is a larger piece carved from a slightly convex block of creamy marble and more complicated in that it contains the first statement of the major preoccupation of the whole of Michelangelo's art: the male nude in movement. Both Condivi and Vasari say that the subject was suggested by Poliziano, but they disagree on what it was, though the nearest identification is the story from Ovid's *Metamorphoses* Book XII, which recounts how the Centaurs, inflamed by wine at the wedding feast of Perithous and the Lapith princess Hippodameia, seized the bride and the other women and attempted to make off with them. In the struggling mêlée of figures Perithous tries to rescue his bride, while Theseus is about to throw a rock at the infuriated Centaur. The rest of the block is filled with a tangle of bodies and is far more reminiscent of a Roman battle sarcophagus than of the often suggested
12 model of the bronze relief of a *Battle of Horsemen* which Bertoldo made about 1475 and which was in the Medici palace. The Bertoldo has no central narrative content, being a continuous relief of fighting men and horsemen each of which is much smaller in proportion to the size of the field, and more scattered. Besides the influence of Bertoldo (who died in December 1491),
11 there is also the influence of the Pisani, father and son, whose pulpits in Pisa (Baptistery and Cathedral), Pistoia (S. Andrea) and Siena (Cathedral) have large reliefs packed with figures, in layers one above the other and also entangled with one another, and these might have provided a stimulus – if one could be certain that Michelangelo had by this time journeyed to these places. That he knew the Pisa pulpits can be inferred from later works but not necessarily from this one. According to Condivi the relief was executed immediately before Lorenzo de' Medici's death in April 1492. Its unfinished

14 MICHELANGELO? *Crucifix*

state may well be because when Lorenzo died Michelangelo returned to his father's house and may have abandoned working on it; it remained in his possession to the end of his life.

When Lorenzo de' Medici died, Michelangelo turned to studying anatomy at the Hospital of Sto Spirito, whose prior apparently allowed him the privilege of dissecting corpses. It is untrue that dissection was forbidden by the Church; what was forbidden was to obtain corpses by digging them up. As a thank-offering for this concession, so vital to his knowledge and understanding of the human frame, Michelangelo is said to have made a *Crucifix*, recorded by Condivi. One was recently discovered in the monastery of Sto Spirito which in its gentleness and smoothness runs counter to the general tenor of the artist's works, and many have been happy

14

to reject it, and to assign it to a date in the 1530s as a work dependent on forms and proportions deriving from the style of Pontormo; but in its favour it must be remembered that it was actually discovered in the monastery, and that its thinness in technique and sweetness of feeling could be accounted for by its being a polychromed wood-carving. What is difficult to understand is that a crucifix by Michelangelo, recorded as having stood on the high altar of Sto Spirito until about 1600, should have been replaced by one by such a lesser artist as Caccini and should, despite Michelangelo's undimmed fame, have disappeared without trace.

In 1493 Michelangelo bought a large block of marble to carve a figure after his own fancy; this must have been the over life-size *Hercules* which belonged to Filippo Strozzi and which originally stood in the courtyard of the Strozzi palace before it went to Fontainebleau in 1529. Michelangelo had known Filippo Strozzi from childhood and his younger brother worked in Strozzi's wool business. All that is known of the *Hercules* is from an engraving by Israel Silvestre of the Jardin de l'Etang at Fontainebleau, where it was the centre-piece before it disappeared in 1713, when the garden was reconstructed.

From 1492 onwards Florence had ceased to be a quiet and self-contained city. Savonarola had begun preaching soon after his return to the city in 1490, and in 1491 he was made Prior of S. Marco. Even before Lorenzo's death his sermons were full of denunciations of the state of the Church, and after the advent to power of Lorenzo's son Piero, his preaching took on an even more apocalyptic tone. He attracted an enormous following, and his terrible denunciations of vice and frivolity, of the characters of the rulers of Florence and of the pope in Rome – Alexander VI Borgia, elected in 1492 – his demands for reform and his prophecies of the dire retribution soon to fall upon the city for its sins, threw everyone into a state of consternation bordering upon panic. The position was made worse by the consequences of a secret treaty made in 1492 between Piero de' Medici and Ferrante of Naples for the dismemberment of Milan. In a misguided move of what he believed would be self-defence, Ludovico Sforza of Milan, regent for his inadequate nephew Giangaleazzo, attempted to divert his enemies' attention by inviting Charles VIII of France to resume French claims to the throne of Naples, once held by the dynasty of Charles of Anjou. Charles VIII, young and ambitious, arrived in north Italy with a large army in September 1494; he met virtually no resistance and Florence, which had always had a strong pro-French party, encouraged him and promised assistance. By mid-October Charles had crossed the Apennines from Piacenza and was encamped before the Florentine fortress of Sarzana. On 9 November Piero de' Medici came to his camp and surrendered to him all the Florentine fortresses. The result was

15 MICHELANGELO *Angel bearing a Candlestick* 1495

disastrous. When Piero returned to Florence and informed the Signoria of the terms he had concluded, the city rose against him in fury at the disgrace. Help was one thing; abject surrender was another. Piero fled and the Medici palace was sacked, but when Charles appeared before the walls of Florence the city had no choice but to admit him. He was in fact welcomed with jubilation, a jubilation tempered by the dismay caused by the size of his army, the disciplined and warlike nature of his troops, the large contingent of Swiss mercenaries, and the amount of exceedingly purposeful-looking artillery.

Long before the French entered Florence Michelangelo had left the city. Before 14 October 1494 he had already gone to Venice – the traditional city of refuge – and from there back to Bologna. Why, it is impossible to be certain. Condivi tells a wild tale about a musician in Piero de' Medici's household who had a dream in which Lorenzo bade him warn Piero of the

16 MICHELANGELO *St Petronius* 1495

impending expulsion of the Medici from Florence, and recounts that when Piero laughed the man to scorn Michelangelo believed him and secretly left the city. People have done strange things for less reason; apprehension caused by Savonarola's violent diatribes, combined with the fact that he had once been an inmate of Lorenzo's household and had been restored to that position after the frivolous Piero had ordered him to make a snowman in the palace courtyard, may well have made Michelangelo believe that discretion was the better part of valour in so dangerous and profitless a connection. In Bologna he found employment in making three figures, Sts Petronius and Proculus, and an angel bearing a candlestick, for the Shrine of St Dominic in

17 MICHELANGELO *St Proculus*
1495

S. Domenico, which Niccolò dell'Arca had left unfinished at his death in March 1494.

The figures are small – on the turn of 2 ft (0·6 m) high, and the angel even less – but they exhibit striking differences in technique. The little angel *15* is rendered with a tender softness of almost waxen quality allied to a largeness in the forms which differentiate it sharply and probably deliberately from the greater particularization of Niccolò's corresponding angel. Oddly, the insides of the wings of Michelangelo's angel are not carved at all. The two saints are quite different: they show a detailed realism which *16, 17* closely resembles the style of the Griffoni Chapel altarpiece once in S.

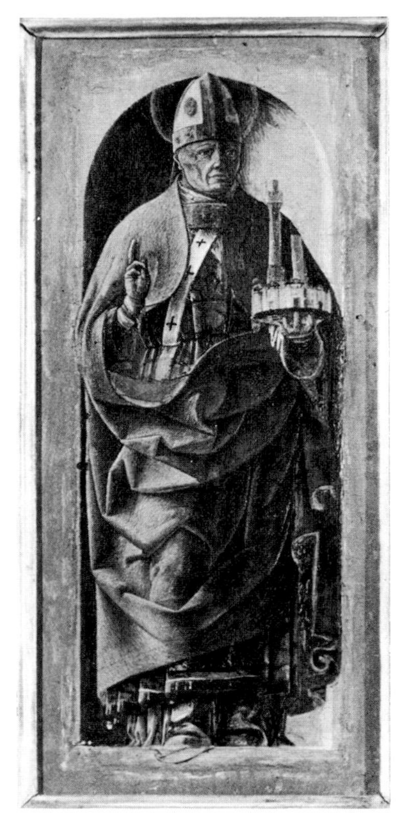

18 ERCOLE DE' ROBERTI *St Petronius* 1475

19 FRANCESCO DEL COSSA *St Florian* 1473

18 Petronio. This work included the *St Petronius* by Ercole de' Roberti, which is as likely to have served as a model for Michelangelo's figure as the *26* della Quercia *St Petronius* on the façade of S. Petronio. The altarpiece *19* also contained a *St Florian* by Cossa whose harsh features and tense energy – as well as its dress – may well have inspired the St Proculus. It has been suggested* that Michelangelo made the angel in deliberate imitation of the mid-thirteenth-century reliefs by Pisan sculptors which formed the earliest part of the shrine, and thus effected both a contrast with the latest work by Niccolò dell'Arca and an assimilation to the older Tuscan reliefs. His propensity for skilful imitation of older works is commented on by his biographers, and would also explain why the two saints are so close to the style of painters popular in Bologna. These strong stylistic differences may, of course, be due as much to the demands of the commissioner, wanting the familiar rather than trusting to a young, untried and unknown sculptor.

The stylistic affinities which the two saints exhibit also suggest that Michelangelo's journey to Venice had taken him through Ferrara, where the

*Alison Luchs, 'Michelangelo's Bologna Angel', in *The Burlington Magazine*, April 1978.

experience of Cosmè Tura's great polyptychs would have introduced him not only to the painter's sculptural treatment of forms and particularly to his handling of drapery, but also to Tura's use of the *Pietà* theme, for instance in the crowning lunette (Paris, Louvre) of the Roverella altarpiece once in S. Giorgio at Ferrara, or in the little version of the same theme (Venice, Museo Correr) from an unknown location. Ercole de' Roberti also used the theme in the predella of the altarpiece of the high altar of S. Giovanni in Monte in Bologna, which consisted of a series of scenes from the Life of Christ in which the *Pietà* was once the central panel. These versions of a theme uncommon in Italian art, but frequent in German sculpture as the *Vesperbild* (of which an example actually existed in S. Domenico), are found among the Ferrarese painters working either in Ferrara or in Bologna, whereas the usual Venetian or the Donatellesque versions of the subject are of the type in which the dead Christ is supported in the tomb by angels – the *Imago Pietatis*. They were to bear fruit in the great *Pietà* executed in Rome four years later, just as the marvellous panels by Jacopo della Quercia now round the portal of S. Petronio, and the *Madonna and Child* and *St Petronius* now over the door, must have been known to Michelangelo, although only the doorway had been completed at the time of this visit, or his later one in 1506.

20
21
22
24, 23
25
28
26

20 Cosmè Tura *Pietà c.* 1474

21 Cosmè Tura *Pietà c.* 1472?

22 Ercole de' Roberti *Pietà*

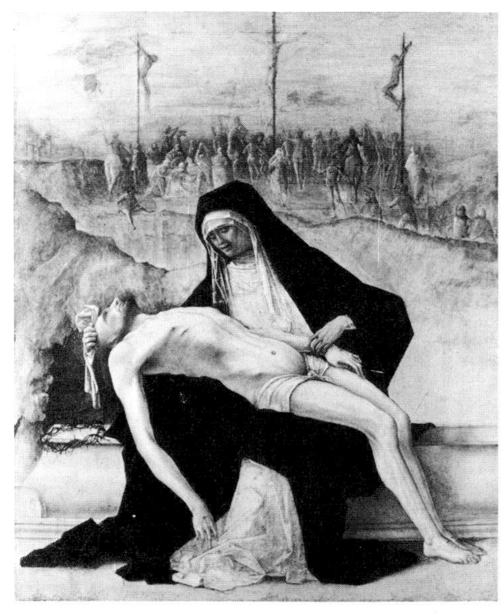

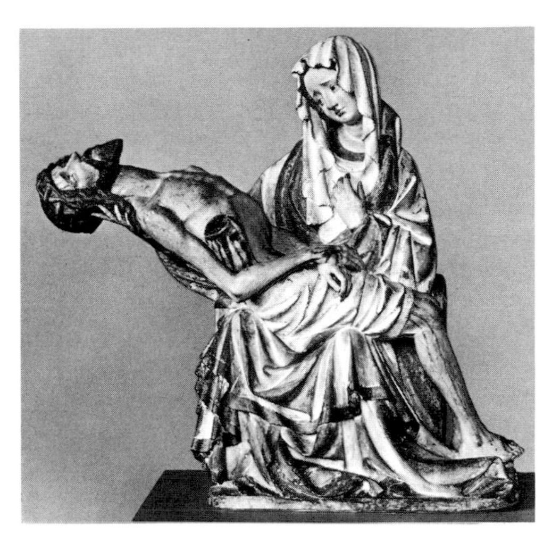

23 German School *Pietà* 14th century

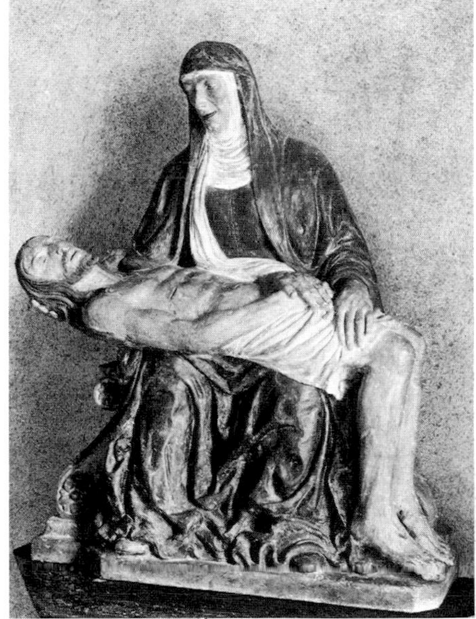

24 Niccolò dell'Arca *Pietà* 1480s?

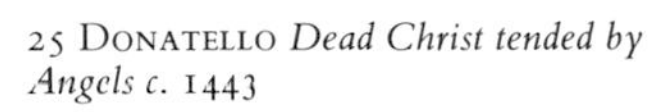

25 Donatello *Dead Christ tended by Angels c.* 1443

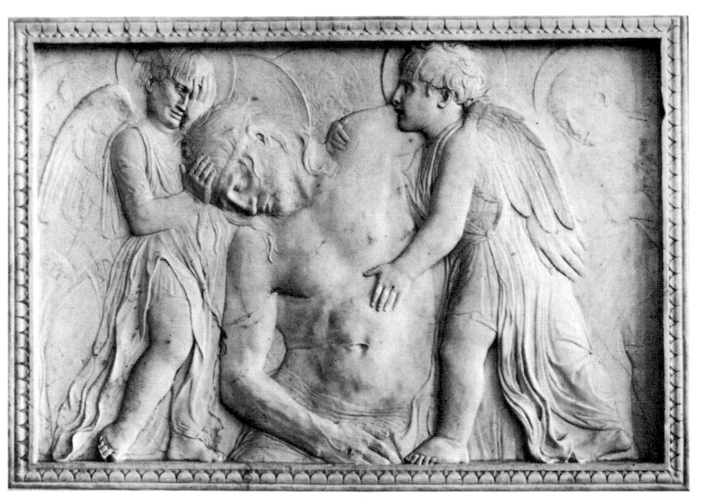

26 Jacopo della Quercia *Madonna and Child* and *St Petronius* 1425–34

After the expulsion of the Medici from Florence and the city's welcome to Charles VIII, the French king pursued his victorious route through Italy. Alexander VI had no option but to grant him free passage through the Papal States and Charles occupied Rome on Christmas Day 1494. He continued on his way to Naples, stopping only to destroy the fortress of Monte S. Giovanni and to kill all its inhabitants – an act of terrorism which inspired such fear that, panic-stricken, King Alfonso abdicated and fled, and the French entered Naples unopposed. From February 1495 onwards they enjoyed the fruits of their victory, and, after having himself crowned king in May 1495, Charles began the journey home, leaving half his army behind as a garrison. Meanwhile, realizing what they had done by helping him, all his former allies had formed a league against him. Charles reached Fornovo, near Parma, and there fought a major but indecisive battle against an army commanded by Federigo Gonzaga of Mantua, the most famous *condottiere* in Italy. Charles extricated himself with the loss of all his baggage and loot;

Gonzaga remained in possession of the field and claimed the victory. By detaching Ludovico Sforza from the league against him Charles managed to reach France, but his garrison in Naples was unable to hold either the city or the province, and had totally capitulated by June 1496. The French invasion thus petered out, but it left great problems behind it. It demonstrated the ease with which small states jealous of each other and incapable of taking anything but the most short-sighted view of their immediate profit could be induced to ally themselves with an invader; it left bitter internecine strife behind; but the most terrible lesson of all was that Italy was utterly vulnerable to any foreign power determined enough to conquer her.

Michelangelo was back in Florence probably by the winter of 1495. Savonarola was now in full power, for though he established a Great Council on the Venetian pattern, he was able to control men and events by the sermons he preached, and by the fears and emotions he aroused. A religious dictatorship, particularly one which encouraged the destruction of 'vanities', condemned the nude and rejected antiquity, hardly provided much opportunity for a sculptor seeking a reputation. A Medici cousin, Lorenzo di Pierfrancesco, who had been one of Botticelli's patrons, commissioned a young *St John the Baptist* (a 'Giovannino') which has been tentatively identified with a figure of the young *Baptist* in the Bargello, recorded in Medici inventories from about 1704 onwards, but always as by Donatello. Its rejection from the canon of Donatello's works began in the late nineteenth century, but it is only recently that an attribution to Michelangelo has been advanced. The rigidity of the pose, the slightly awkward stance, the rather hard features and the arbitrary handling of the hair of the head and the goatskin clothing of the figure, while they suggest the work of an inexperienced sculptor, cannot very convincingly be related to the work Michelangelo had already done in Florence and Bologna.

The same patron also suggested that a nude *Sleeping Cupid* would sell at a higher price if it were made to look like an antique, and a dealer sold it in Rome for far more than Michelangelo had been paid for it. Condivi tells a confused story connecting the *Cupid* with Michelangelo's first Roman patron, Cardinal Riario, who apparently bought it as an antique and then furiously rejected it when its modern authorship was disclosed by Michelangelo himself. It was certainly in Urbino in 1502, since Isabella d'Este wrote to her brother Cardinal Ippolito asking him to persuade Cesare Borgia, who had treacherously captured Urbino, to sell her the statue at the very moment when she was giving refuge to the Duke and Duchess of Urbino in the palace at Mantua. Borgia obliged her, and eventually the *Cupid* came to England with the Mantua Collection when Charles I bought it in 1631, only to disappear at the Commonwealth sales of royal property.

Partly through indignation at being cheated, partly in search of work, Michelangelo arrived in Rome on 25 June 1496, with a letter of introduction from Lorenzo di Pierfrancesco to Cardinal Riario. Although both Condivi and Vasari declare that the cardinal commissioned nothing from him, this is contradicted by a letter from Michelangelo to his father, dated 1 July 1497, in which he explains his delay in returning to Florence: 'I have not yet been able to settle up my affairs with the Cardinal and I do not want to leave without . . . being remunerated for my labours.' Since both biographers state that the banker Jacopo Galli, the cardinal's near neighbour at the Riario palace (which later became the Cancelleria), commissioned an *Eros* and a *Bacchus*, the possibility is that one of these may have originally been destined for the cardinal, who possibly relinquished it to his friend, since he apparently had little taste for 'modern' antiques.

27 Of the two statues for Galli, the *Bacchus* alone survives, and was placed in Galli's garden among his collection of Roman statues and fragments, for it was drawn there by Maerten van Heemskerck between 1532 and 1535, mutilated by the removal of an arm, apparently to make it look more antique. It is an astonishing work for a man of twenty-one. Life-sized, his plump, smooth body entirely nude, his head garlanded with fruiting vines, the god gazes with unfocused eyes at the wine-cup he lifts unsteadily before him, swaying tipsily as he tries to hold his balance, while the leopard-skin slips from his nerveless fingers and the little satyr nibbling at the grapes grins mischievously behind his back. In a sense, this is the first Mannerist statue, since it is conceived not just in the round and free-standing; the irregular circle of the plinth, and the position of the satyr, invite one to walk round the statue and to view it from all sides, all points of view being equally valid. The surface has weathered, since the statue stood out of doors, but the abrasion of the marble does not disguise the intense naturalism of the treatment of forms and details. The *Bacchus* competes with the antique on its own terms as a representation of the male nude, but at the same time it invites a moral as well as an intellectual and spiritual judgment. It is the unregenerate soul gazing at the uplifted cup of wine with unseeing eyes, unable to recognize its significance. It is the expression of untrammelled natural desire, swayed by passions, since in Renaissance Platonic philosophy the body is the prison of the soul, and drunkenness implies the enslavement of the soul by physical desires and vices, and its debasement by the rejection of spiritual values. In its overpowering of reason by physical means it is the antithesis of the Divine afflatus of spiritual ecstasy. The *Bacchus* thus expresses ideas far beyond its exploitation of antique prototypes.

As early as 18 November 1497 the French Cardinal Jean Bilhères de Lagraulas (referred to in Italian accounts of his curial career as Cardinal de la

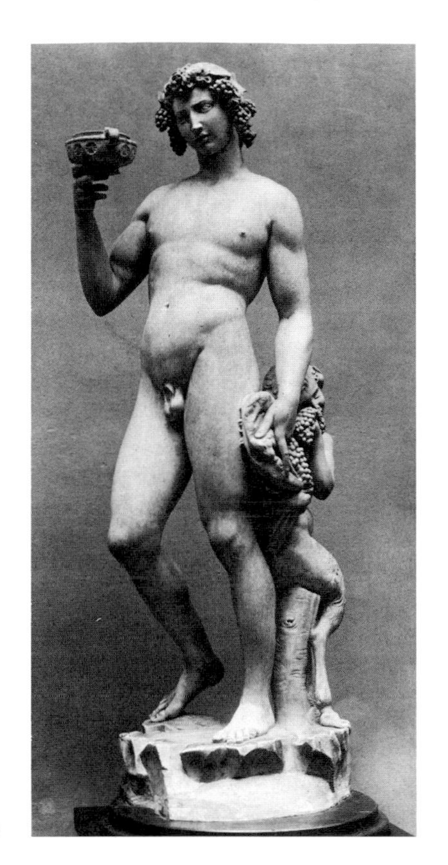

27 MICHELANGELO *Bacchus c.* 1497/98

Groslaie) had decided to commission a *Pietà* for his tomb, for at this time he wrote to ask for facilities for Michelangelo to obtain marble from Carrara. Michelangelo was in Carrara in March and April 1498, and a contract for the group was made on 27 August 1498, with Jacopo Galli as agent, which specifics the subject as a *Pietà* and defines exactly what that means, as if the subject were obscure, which, since this is a very early sculptural rendering of the theme in Italy, it may well have been. Painted examples existed, such as those by the Ferrarese artists mentioned earlier, and *20–22* sculpture groups of the *Pietà* were common in Germany and in France, *23, 24* where the theme of the Suffering Christ was popular, particularly for tombs. Variants of the subject became popular in Florentine painting in the same decade, as is evidenced – among other examples – by Perugino's group of about 1495 (Florence, Uffizi) in which the dead Christ lies across His mother's knees, though this example evades the problems of proportions by having Christ's head and feet supported by an angel and the Magdalen, and by the two versions of the subject by Botticelli (Munich, Alte Pinakothek; Milan, Poldi Pezzoli), both probably painted about the turn of the century, and expressing a more strident and agonized grief than is to be found in Perugino's placid regret and Michelangelo's noble resignation.

28 Michelangelo's triumph is that he transformed the northern theme while retaining its tragedy and pathos, and the clumsy groups with their uncertain management of the comparative sizes of the Virgin and her dead Son become in his hands the supreme expression of sacrifice, resignation and aesthetic beauty. He was inspired by Quercia's bulky and timeless draperies, and by Leonardo's concentration on the meaningful relationship of figures, to enlarge the mass of draperies over the Virgin's knees into a pedestal for the limp body of the dead Christ, so that she who gave Him birth becomes the altar on which His Sacrifice is offered – God's surrender of Himself to be martyred by man. The major forms are modelled with precision: the drooping arm, the dangling legs, the twisted torso, are treated with exact anatomical knowledge yet with infinite feeling. The minor forms of head and face are detailed with decisiveness, and are even a trifle thin and pinched. The head of the Virgin, made bigger by the bulk of her veil, has delicate and clear-cut features, and the criticism that she looked too young to be the mother of a man of thirty-three was countered by Michelangelo's own argument that her purity and virginity prolonged her youth and arrested the normal processes of decay, so that in the words of St Bernard's prayer in Dante's *Paradiso*:

Virgin Mother, daughter of your Son,
Lowly yet exalted above all creatures,
Fixed goal of the eternal will,
You are the one who so ennobled human nature
That its Creator did not disdain
To make Himself its creation.

The group was to be finished in one year, but Cardinal de la Groslaie died in August 1499, possibly before the work was finished. He was buried, as the chief representative of the French Crown at the Vatican, in the chapel of S. Petronilla (the Chapel of the Kings of France) and the *Pietà* was placed over his tomb. When the chapel was demolished with the old basilica to make way for Michelangelo's new St Peter's, the group was moved; its present location, in the first chapel on the right of Maderno's extended nave, was arranged in 1749. Recent vandalism has made it essential to protect the *Pietà* with glass screens. It is Michelangelo's only signed work: on the ribbon which holds the mass of draperies over Mary's breast are the words MICHAEL · AĞELUS · BONAROTUS · FLORENTIN · FACIEBAT. As a work of art it remains the supreme statement of a theme which many sculptors have

28 MICHELANGELO *Pietà* 1497–1500

endeavoured to equal but none has ever surpassed. It also represents, despite the slight reminiscences of Verrocchio in the treatment of the features, a complete break with the past. Such is the mastery of its execution, the splendour of its imaginative power, the finality of its statement, that it represents, even more than the *Bacchus*, and as much as Leonardo's *Last Supper* in Milan, the end of the Early Renaissance in Italian art and the beginning of a new artistic age.

In Florence, political events had taken a tragic turn. Savonarola, after establishing his oppressive 'Theocracy' and successfully defeating in 1497 an ill-managed attempt to restore Piero de' Medici, overreached himself and fell from power in April 1498. After a trial made into a hideous travesty of justice by confessions extracted under torture, he and two companions were condemned, hanged, and their bodies burnt. In the same month Charles VIII of France died and was succeeded by his cousin Louis XII, who, among his titles, assumed those of the Kingdom of the Two Sicilies (i.e. Naples) and the Duchy of Milan, claiming the last through his grandmother, a Visconti princess, despite the Salic Law which barred succession in the female line. Both Florence and Venice were pro-French at this moment, and the Venetians suggested to Louis than an alliance with them would help his claims against Milan and Naples. The lessons of 1496 had already been forgotten. In July 1499 the French army crossed the Alps, taking fortress after fortress as it advanced. Ludovico Sforza fled to his overlord, the Emperor Maximilian, and on 6 September the citadel of Milan surrendered to the French. Louis XII arrived in Milan in triumph in October, escorted by a glittering cohort of Italian princely allies, French cardinals and diplomatic envoys.

Alexander VI then allowed Cesare Borgia to carve a personal dukedom for himself out of papal territories in the Romagna, and with French troops Cesare fought a devastating campaign against Pesaro, Imola, Forlì, Faenza and other towns which had been pro-Sforza. In January 1500 Cesare's French troops were recalled. Ludovico had invaded Lombardy with an army of German and Swiss mercenaries, and the Milanese, sick of French extortion, had rebelled. The French lost Lombardy as quickly as they had won it, but Louis immediately dispatched another army, and in April he fought a decisive battle at Novara, which he won because Ludovico's unpaid Swiss mercenaries refused to fight against their compatriots in the French army. Ludovico was taken prisoner and ended his days in a French prison; Louis reoccupied Lombardy.

In October 1500 Cesare completed his campaign of conquest and in 1501 the pope made him Duke of Romagna. It had always been papal policy that no foreign power should occupy Naples, but by a secret treaty made in June 1501 Alexander reversed this policy and agreed to the division of Naples between Spain and France, in order to checkmate his unruly Roman barons, particularly the Colonna family, who were always supported by an anti-papal Naples. The French, encamped outside Rome, were joined by Cesare, and their sudden violent invasion was unopposed. Federigo of Naples fled and then surrendered to the French who compensated him with a dukedom and divided his country with Spain. The Colonna were excommunicated and all their possessions were confiscated, some being given to the Orsini, their bitter rivals, but the major part going to the Borgia family. Cesare restarted his campaigns of territorial acquisition, attacked Urbino without warning in June 1502, and after the capture of Senigaglia on 31 December 1502 he suddenly seized all his generals, who were plotting to destroy him because they now realized that no one was safe from him. He executed them all including an Orsini, while in Rome Alexander arrested all the Orsini he could find. Cesare devastated the Orsini lands and attacked their stronghold of Bracciano. Its defender appealed to the French for help, but to no avail since they had now fallen out with their Spanish allies, and on 16 May Gonsalvo de Cordoba took Naples from them. Cesare was negotiating with the Emperor for Pisa, Lucca and Siena as fiefs, and his troops had just captured Perugia, when he and his father both contracted virulent malaria at the same time in Rome. On 18 August 1503 Alexander VI died.

Cesare was too ill to move, but at the beginning of September the College of Cardinals, fearing possible armed interference with the Conclave, insisted that he should leave Rome. The Conclave resulted in the election of the old and ailing Pius III – a stop-gap pope – but when Cesare returned to Rome his private army had dwindled from 12,000 to 650 men. In the face of mounting demands for his trial he tried to escape, and he was forced eventually to take refuge in the Castel S. Angelo from the fury of the Orsini. Pius III died on 18 October, having been pope for less than a month; the new pope, elected in a one-day Conclave on 31 October 1503, was Julius II. His first tasks were to restore order in Rome, to get rid of Cesare Borgia, to recover the papal lands alienated by Alexander VI, and to prevent Venice from grabbing the papal fiefs in the Romagna on the excuse that she was liberating them from Borgia rule. On 28 December came the news that the French had been totally routed by Gonsalvo de Cordoba on the banks of the Garigliano, and the French had lost all Naples for good.

Cesare abandoned his claims in the Romagna, and in April 1504 he was given a safe conduct by Gonsalvo de Cordoba, but when he arrived in Naples he was arrested and sent to a fortress in Spain. Thus the Borgia vanished from the Italian scene. Cesare escaped in October 1506 to the safety of his brother-in-law's court of Navarre, and in May 1507 he was killed during a border skirmish. He was thirty-one, and his meteoric career had lasted just fifteen years.

During these eventful years Florence had been protected from conquest by the French alliance. After the death of Savonarola, republican government was restored, and rule by the reconstituted Great Council involved new office-holders every two months, which meant a complete change of government six times a year. When Cesare Borgia invaded Florentine territory in 1502 Florence appealed to Louis who, while he was quite willing that Cesare should conquer any parts of the peninsula which he did not himself want, was determined that territories which he required as a compliant base for his own operations should be respected. French troops were sent to Tuscany; Cesare allowed the Florentines to buy him off and withdrew.

But the frightening episode bore fruit. It was decided that as well as the Venetian system of the Grand Council it would be a more effective form of government to adopt also the Venetian system of a single head of state, and on 1 November 1502 Piero Soderini was elected Gonfalonier for life. He was a modest, moderate, competent man, who restored the finances of the city, and he was greatly helped by the removal of the threat of insurrection periodically fomented by the irresponsible Piero de' Medici, through the latter's death at the Battle of Garigliano. The fortunes of the Medici family were now in the skilful hands of Cardinal Giovanni, Lorenzo the Magnificent's son, and of Giulio, Lorenzo's nephew, both later destined to become pope, both intelligent men who realized that conquest by invasion or revolt was unlikely to regain them their lost patrimony.

Nor were all these complex political events without their repercussions on the arts. The French invasion of 1499, which destroyed the Sforza court in Milan, drove out both Bramante and Leonardo. Bramante settled in Rome, where he was working from about 1500 onwards; Leonardo, after making brief journeys to Mantua and Venice, returned to Florence in 1500 and then became military engineer to Cesare Borgia. The fall of his patron brought him back to Florence in 1503. Just as the declining fortunes of the Medici had provoked Michelangelo into leaving Florence in 1494, so the political opportunism of the Borgia pope left so little prospect of serious patronage in Rome that it must have contributed to his decision to return to Florence in the spring of 1501, probably in May.

Michelangelo returned preceded by his reputation, acknowledged already as the foremost sculptor of his day. In August 1501 the Operai dell'Opera del Duomo – the board of works of the cathedral – decided to confer on

Michelangelo the large block of marble which Agostino di Duccio or his assistant had in the 1460s so badly botched that work on the gigantic figure which was to be made from it, destined for one of the buttresses of the three apses of the cathedral, had had to be abandoned. In 1476 Antonio Rossellino had been commissioned to execute the statue, but he did nothing. From the block, Michelangelo carved the *David*. When it was finished in 1504, the commission appointed to decide where the statue should be placed judged that the best position for it would be the site where Donatello's *Judith* then stood, in front of the Palazzo della Signoria, and not on or in front of the cathedral. One of the important considerations in the choice of a site for the *David* was that as a result of damage from the attempts which previous men had made to carve from the block Michelangelo's figure is very narrow when seen from the side. It was essential that it should be placed against a wall, so as to display the figure in width rather than to encourage an all-round view. *32*

For the Florentines, David represented the essence of civic virtue – courage, fortitude, faith – just as Judith was the symbol of the victory of courage over tyranny in the struggle for freedom, so that Michelangelo's gigantic figure came eventually to have both connotations. The *David* has a

29 Donatello *David* 1450s

30 Andrea del Verrocchio *David c.* 1473/75

31 Nicola Pisano *Fortitude* 1260

32 (*right*) Michelangelo *David* 1501–04

long symbolic heritage derived not only from Biblical history but also from the antique in its echoes of Hercules triumphing through strength over the labours inflicted upon him by tyranny, and an uncanny but surely not accidental parallel can be found for it in Nicola Pisano's figure in the Pisa Baptistery, where Fortitude in the guise of Hercules supports one of the angles of the pulpit – becomes, that is, one of the cornerstones of Faith. Stylistically, it is as much a new departure as the *Pietà* in Rome had been: a new statement of an old theme, given a new monumentality.

31

There were plenty of artistic precedents for Michelangelo to follow had he wished – Donatello's bronze *David* stood in the courtyard of the Medici palace, and Verrocchio's bronze *David* had apparently also been made for the Medici, though its original site is unknown. He followed none of these. His David is no longer a boy calm yet triumphant and touched with glory, but a youth full of latent energy and strength, with huge limbs and a watchful, uncertain expression on his sharply delineated features. One massive hand dangles against his right thigh, the other is raised to hold the sling, so that the long line of the open left-hand silhouette contrasts with the closed forms on

29 *30*

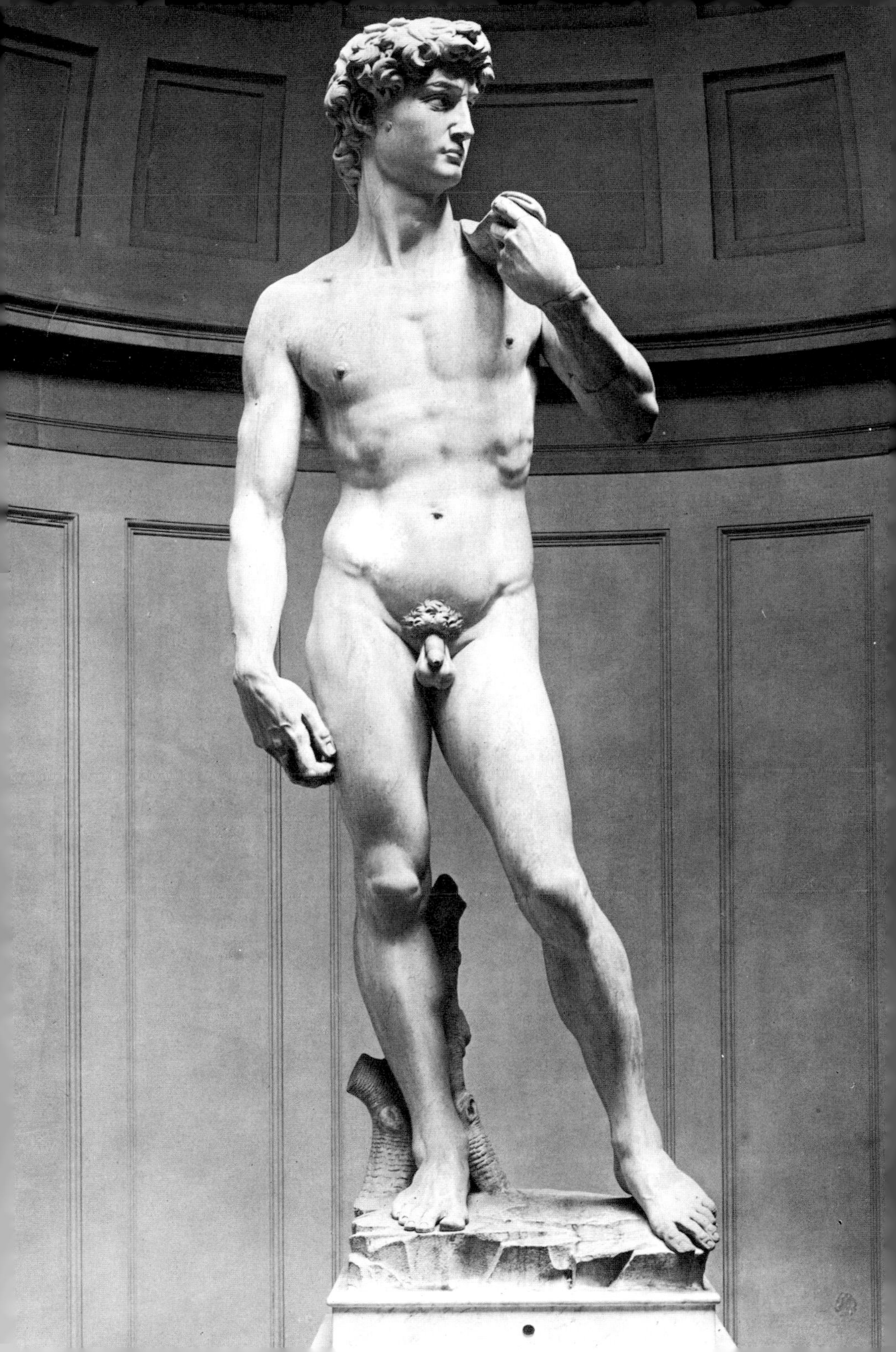

the right, and expresses the medieval concept of the open and vulnerable passive side, opposed by the closely defended active side, while the head is turned to look in the direction from which attack may come. This is not the victorious David of Donatello or Verrocchio, since there is no decapitated head of a defeated enemy between his feet, no sword of victory in his hand. This is the David of watchfulness, faith and hope: 'The Lord is my light and my salvation; whom shall I fear? In thee, O Lord, do I put my trust, for thou art my rock and my fortress.' These were overtones which must have echoed with a familiar yet fearful ring in the ears of men who had listened to Savonarola's sermons, known the misery of invasion and the terrors of Cesare Borgia's threats, and had experienced the bitterness and disillusion of the past years and feared still for the future. In its attitude of quiet and watchful anticipation, the *David* was a clear and telling symbol of the men who erected it in pride of place before their seat of government.

When Michelangelo reached Florence in 1501, he found an artistic giant in the centre of the stage. Leonardo had returned, after his long Milanese absence, in April 1500, and in April 1501 he exhibited a cartoon for an altarpiece of the *Madonna and Child with St Anne*. A contemporary description of this cartoon, by Isabella d'Este's agent in Florence, Fra Pietro da Novellara, is the major cause of argument whether the *Virgin and Child with St Anne* in the Louvre or the *Virgin and Child with St Anne and St John* in the National Gallery, London, is to be identified with it. Novellara's description says that the Christ Child is restrained by His mother from grasping the lamb; Vasari's description mentions an infant St John, and no St John appears in the Louvre version. Novellara's description has also been held to justify the existence of a third (now lost) cartoon, because he says that the figures are turned to the left – but whose left, his or the figures' within the picture? In both cartoons the figures are turned to our right. There is no doubt, however, that stylistically the London cartoon is the earlier work. Vasari also says that the cartoon exhibited in Florence later went to France, but he does not say when; the fact that he says that it included an infant St John suggests that he had fairly accurate information, and it would have been within the memory of many of his friends and informants in Florence. Whatever the answer to the problem, the cartoon created a sensation and was visited, as Vasari records, by streams of admirers, and must have attracted every artist in the city, Michelangelo included, since there is a drawing (Oxford, Ashmolean) by him which, though it clearly is only inspired by Leonardo, yet proves how much impact the older man's work made on him. The repercussions of the Leonardo can be seen in four of his works executed in the years immediately following. He also returned to

33

33 LEONARDO DA VINCI *Virgin and Child with St Anne and St John c.* 1500

Florence with a commission from Cardinal Piccolomini (there is a letter written on 22 May 1501 about the work) to execute fifteen statues each about 4 ft (1·2 m) high for the Piccolomini altar in Siena Cathedral, but in the end he was only responsible for four of them, of which only two can be ascribed to Michelangelo himself, the others being done by assistants. He allowed the commission to lapse in 1504, when the four figures were delivered. *34*

During the time that the *David* was being worked on he painted the *Doni Tondo*, probably in 1503 since the picture is associated with the marriage of Angelo Doni to Maddalena Strozzi, which took place either late in 1503 or early in 1504, and he carved the *Bruges Madonna*, the *Taddei Tondo* and the *Pitti Tondo*. There is also the mysterious *Manchester Madonna* and a lost bronze *David*, since one is recorded as having been made for Pierre de Rohan, Maréchal de Gié, between 1502 and 1508 (it was finished by Benedetto da Rovezzano). Benedetto Varchi in 1564 described it as having been made not in imitation of the Donatello in the courtyard of the Medici palace so much as in competition with it. This suggests that the tiny sketch in

35 the Louvre, which is a study for the marble David's arm and shows another figure of David with the head of Goliath at his feet, may be the record of this figure, which went to France and disappeared there after 1650.

36 The *Bruges Madonna* was acquired in 1503–04 by a Flemish cloth merchant called Mouscron (Moscheroni), who placed it on the altar where it still stands in Notre-Dame in Bruges. In letters written from Rome in 1505–06 Michelangelo betrayed great anxiety over the possibility that his father, who was to pack and dispatch the work, might allow anyone to see it; hence the conjecture that it may have been part of the Piccolomini altar, and that Michelangelo feared he might be accused of bad faith in selling the statue elsewhere when Pius III – the commissioning cardinal became pope in 1503 – died within a month of his election. It must, however, have been known,

34 MICHELANGELO *St Peter*, Piccolomini altar 1501–04

35 MICHELANGELO Drawing for bronze and marble *Davids c.* 1501/02

since its repercussions on the young Raphael are clear. Eventually, the statue was sent to Bruges in 1506. Stylistically, it can be attached to the St Peter's *Pietà*, through the grave, frontal figure of the Virgin, the closeness of her physical type to the Virgin of the *Pietà*, the way in which her heavy drapery *28* envelops and forms a podium for the body of the Christ Child, standing between her knees in an easy relaxed pose. Although Mouscron did not negotiate to buy the group until 1503, it is more than probable that Michelangelo began it as early as 1501, since the similarity of the Virgin to the Virgin of the *Pietà*, and the high degree of finish, suggest that her figure was begun at least then, even if the Christ Child would fit better with the final date of about 1504.

The *Taddei Tondo* and the *Pitti Tondo* are both marble reliefs of the circular type familiar for generations on tombs, but neither had such an end in view. Both appear to have been 'virtuoso' works, executed for patrons who were admirers. Both are unfinished, either because Michelangelo's departure for Rome in 1505 prevented him from completing them, or perhaps deliberately in that the adumbrated forms confer an additional poetry on the concept. The *Taddei Tondo* is of an unusual delicacy and tenderness. The Virgin's *37* head, turned in profile on her shoulders, emerges mistily from the block,

37 MICHELANGELO *Taddei Tondo* 1504–05

wearing the same type of headcloth which totally conceals her hair as is found in both the earlier Virgins; the Christ Child sprawls across her lap shrinking away from the bird which the stalwart little Baptist thrusts at Him, while the Virgin's hand, hardly visible in the roughness of the background, restrains the Baptist gently. Christ's pose has been adapted from a child in the Medea Sarcophagus (Vatican), turned at right angles, but a similar recumbent Christ Child had already appeared in Leonardo's *Madonna and Child with St Anne* cartoon, though with an entirely different gesture and *33*

36 MICHELANGELO *Bruges Madonna* 1503–04

significance. Michelangelo's use of a classical prototype may have been for the very purpose of avoiding direct imitation of Leonardo's motive. The relief was apparently given by Michelangelo to Taddeo Taddei when he left for Rome.

38 The *Pitti Tondo*, made for Bartolommeo Pitti in the same years, presents rather striking differences. It is much smaller than the *Taddei Tondo*, and much less unfinished, and whereas the group in the *Taddei Tondo* is all enclosed within the block, the head of the Virgin in the *Pitti Tondo* projects above the level of the roundel, and the whole relief is much higher. The figure of the Virgin is much closer to that of a prophetess or a sibyl, and the rather tense, crouching pose is more alert, more compressed in energy than that of the Taddei Virgin. The Christ Child leans on the book on her lap, and she holds Him loosely, while the faintly delineated Baptist glances over her shoulder, emerging from the rough claw-hatching of the unfinished background. The type of the Virgin's head is fuller, more rounded than either the *Bruges Madonna* or the *Taddei Tondo* type, the features less pinched. Both these roundels show Michelangelo's technique at its most interesting: the use of the claw chisel, with which the blocks are worked, is infinitely delicate yet firm, so that despite their unfinished state every form is fully realized, fully developed. Perhaps also these reliefs were instructive to him in the degree to which lack of total finish could help, rather than hinder, the realization of form and feeling.

39 The third tondo is the one painted for the Doni family in, probably, 1503: a painting, not a sculpture, and the only datable painting by Michelangelo before the Sistine Ceiling. Clearly, it too was influenced by the great groups by Leonardo, not in design but through Michelangelo's immediate comprehension of what Leonardo meant by the pyramidal construction of a group of figures in space linked by psychological interaction. The central group is constructed like a piece of sculpture, the colours are hard and bright, the contours firm as tempera painting demands, excluding any use of misty *chiaroscuro* or *sfumato* technique to blur the exact delineation. It is as if Michelangelo were determined to demonstrate that absolute clarity is no bar to the unity and cohesion of a group, and that the technical devices of Leonardo's characteristic handling were at best unnecessary, at worst too redolent of poetic licence. In the foreground, the Virgin reaches over her shoulder to take the Christ Child from Joseph: a tightly knit group, compact as a piece of sculpture. Behind them is a low parapet, marking the middle distance, and immediately behind this barrier the young Baptist looks up towards the Christ Child. Behind the Baptist is a curious ridged rock wall against and upon which two groups of nude youths disport themselves, unheedful of the group in the foreground. The Old Dispensation of

38 MICHELANGELO *Pitti Tondo* 1504–05

unregenerate humanity cannot perceive the total change which the group in the foreground portends; only the Baptist, who in time belongs to the Old Dispensation, is able to see and understand the significance of the group in the foreground to which he is linked by birth and by race. The Mosaic world *sub lege* brings forth and is crowned by, so to speak, the New Dispensation, the world *sub gratia*, represented by the Infant Saviour; the Baptist alone is conscious of being the link between the two worlds.

39 MICHELANGELO *Holy Family (Doni Tondo)* 1503/04

40 Michelangelo *Manchester Madonna*

There is a further painting of the *Madonna and Child with the Infant Baptist* and a frieze of four angels, commonly called the *Manchester Madonna*. This unfinished picture, in tempera on panel, has been much contested and is almost universally rejected as a Michelangelo. If it were by him, then it would have to be very early indeed, most probably belonging to the period between his return from Bologna and his departure for Rome in 1496, since the character of the painting and the hard, linear drawing cannot be fitted in to his later style, even as early as the *Doni Tondo*. The types of the heads resemble those in the *Bruges Madonna* and the two marble reliefs; the assurance of the drawing and the general style of the composition, which is clearly a fifteenth-century not a sixteenth-century work, make it virtually impossible to attribute the painting to any other artist working in Florence at the turn of the century, and it would also appear to precede the impact of Leonardo's more involved form of figure grouping. So one is left with the problem of an unknown master of great ability – a highly unlikely occurrence. Attempts have been made to group other Madonna pictures round this one, but these efforts remain unconvincing.

40

In April 1503 – that is, before the *David* was quite finished – Michelangelo agreed with the Operai del Duomo and the officers of the Wool Guild (who were probably going to find the money) to carve twelve statues of Apostles, one per year. He began the *Matthew* and left it unfinished when he went to Rome in March 1505, but despite the cancellation of the contract at the end of the year, he clearly intended to continue the work when he was in Florence in 1506. The *Matthew* is a massive figure, still enclosed in its block as if struggling like Lazarus to free himself from a winding-sheet; it provides a marvellous lesson in Michelangelo's method as a sculptor, proving that descriptions of his working from the front of the block backwards, revealing the figure little by little as it emerged from the stone, are perfectly accurate. The work was also interrupted by the commission from the Gonfalonier Piero Soderini which involved Michelangelo's painting a Battle Scene in the main hall, the Sala dei Cinquecento, of the Palazzo della Signoria, on the wall flanking that on which Leonardo was to paint the *Battle of Anghiari*. That there was an antipathy between the two men is a commonplace, but it in no way can be held as the cause of the abandonment by both of their work. Leonardo's violent and unusual mêlée of fighting horses and men failed because of the faulty and experimental technique used by an artist untrained in fresco; Michelangelo, after completing probably only a part of the cartoon for the *Battle of Cascina*, was summoned to Rome by Julius II in March 1505 and commissioned to make the pope's tomb.

41

The cartoon for the *Battle of Cascina* (an incident in the Pisan War of 1364) provided Michelangelo with his first great opportunity to display his now

41 MICHELANGELO *St Matthew* 1503–08

unrivalled ability as a draughtsman of nude men in violent action. The actual cartoon is lost – it was dismembered later in the sixteenth century and no part has survived – but we know from a partial copy made about 1542 by Aristotile da Sangallo something of what it looked like. It is also documented that Michelangelo made the cartoon in a room in the Dyers' Hospital (Ospedale dei Tintori), and that it was not transferred to the Council Chamber before 1508, so that there is no reason to believe that the two artists ever met on the site. For the cartoon there are numerous drawings by Michelangelo which are among his most expressive and beautiful works. The portion which Sangallo records was only part of the centre; there were other figures including a group of men and horses for which there are drawings. This would have been essential to fill the space which has been reconstructed by Wilde as measuring about 22 ft by 57 ft 6 in (7 m by 17·5 m), and Wilde also conjectured that other figures, omitted by Sangallo, were in the background.

42

43

In March 1505 Julius II sent for Michelangelo and commissioned the elaborate monument the later history of which Michelangelo described as the 'Tragedy of the Tomb'. His first grandiose project for a free-standing monument was approved in April, and he spent until December in Carrara

42 Aristotile da Sangallo Copy of part of Michelangelo's *Battle of Cascina c.* 1542

43 MICHELANGELO Drawing for the *Battle of Cascina* c. 1504

selecting and preparing the marble for it. When he returned to Rome in January 1506 and went to see the pope to get the money to pay for the marble, he found the whole position had changed; the pope refused to receive him, refused to provide any money, and Michelangelo was expelled from the papal palace with more energy than discretion. Michelangelo blamed Bramante for the disaster. The project for the rebuilding of St Peter's – the basilica was in a ruinous state and partial rebuilding had been going on since the mid-1450s – had now assumed first place in Julius's mind, and on 18 April 1506 a medal was struck to commemorate the laying of the foundation-stone of the new church. But there were other reasons for the difficulties, besides the story Vasari tells of Bramante having persuaded Julius that it was unlucky to have one's tomb made during one's lifetime.

Ever since his election Julius had been fighting, first to recover the cities of the Papal States alienated by Alexander VI to Cesare Borgia, which had been grabbed by Venice on the elimination of Borgia power, and then to reestablish his control over the papal fiefs of Perugia and Bologna, both of which had been taken by force by their former ruling families, the Baglioni and the Bentivogli. The loss of these territories meant the loss of all revenues from them, and the internecine warfare which resulted in the two cities produced clamant refugees who exhorted Julius to intervene. He had no troops, except the Swiss Guards which he founded from two hundred loyal and devoted men, and he was forced to secure himself from his unruly and unreliable feudal barons by using his family in a succession of strategic dynastic marriages. He tried unsuccessfully to obtain French help, but finally he led a campaign in person with a mere handful of men; by early September 1506 he had recovered Perugia, and in November he entered Bologna in triumph. It was more difficult to dislodge the Venetians from the Romagna, since by now Julius had to contend with the double threat of encroachments both territorial and on his papal authority from France and Spain, plus the threat that the Emperor Maximilian would insist on being crowned in Rome and cross the frontier with a large army.

Finally, in December 1508, France, Spain and the Emperor joined together in the League of Cambrai, by which they agreed to divide the mainland territories of Venice between them, and Julius was invited to join so as to recover his Romagna cities. He did so unwillingly, when all other persuasions failed, since the Venetians were filled with totally unjustified confidence in their power to ride out the storm. On 14 May 1509 they were disastrously defeated by the French at the Battle of Agnadello in the Rivolta d'Adda, and their mercenary army immediately deserted them. They sued for peace, gave up the papal territories, released their mainland cities from their allegiance, but the peace terms were so harsh that Julius realized that they meant the destruction of Venice, which was entirely contrary to his own goal of finally ejecting the foreigner from Italy. Even after Venice accepted terms which amounted to a virtual capitulation in February 1510, Julius's troubles were far from over. The Emperor was trying to curtail papal power in Germany so as to reduce the pope to a mere figurehead, the French were attempting to gain control of the whole of the north of Italy, the Spaniards were securely in power in Naples, so that the Papal States were threatened from both north and south by foreign armies. Bologna was again lost in December 1511 because the papal legate proved a worse tyrant than the Bentivogli, and when the losing general, the Duke of Urbino, and the legate met to explain their actions to Julius in Ravenna, during the row that ensued the duke murdered the legate. Julius returned to Rome in June 1511, and though all feared the next move that the King of France would make, surprisingly he retreated, after promoting in May 1511 an anti-papal Council to be held at Pisa. This failed because the majority of bishops summoned to it hesitated to attack the pope in so direct a fashion, and because Julius himself summoned the Lateran Council to meet in April 1512, thus checkmating his opponents.

By now, the French were wearying of their Italian adventures which cost enormous treasure and provided little but empty glory. The Venetians regained their lost territories (they ruled them better), and despite the crushing defeat of the papal armies by the French on Easter Sunday, 11 April 1512, at Ravenna, huge French losses which included their commander, Gaston de Foix, ruled out any follow-up of their victory. The Emperor abandoned them, and allowed Swiss mercenaries to cross his territories on their way to service with the Venetians. French effort faded: they lost Pavia to the Swiss; Milan and Genoa both revolted against them; the Romagna cities returned to their papal allegiance; and Julius recaptured Bologna and took Parma and Piacenza from Milan and added them to the Papal States. The French retreated across the Alps in disarray, and on 23 June 1512 Julius went in triumph to his titular church of S. Pietro in Vincoli to give thanks for being 'freed from chains'.

Part of the general settlement was the unanimous decision that Florence should be punished for being pro-French, for refusing to join the League, and for harbouring the schismatic cardinals who had tried to organize the abortive Council of Pisa. It was decided to restore the Medici, and a combined papal and Spanish army set upon Tuscany. The Spaniards sacked Prato in August 1512, Florence surrendered, and Giulio de' Medici, later cardinal and later still pope as Clement VII, was sent as ruler. But by now Julius himself was failing, sleepless with anxiety over the possibility of new combinations between Spain and France. He was ill by Christmas, and died during the night of 20/21 February 1513.

In view of the background of ceaseless struggle, of lack of money, of his concentration on the urgencies of defending papal authority and restoring his shattered states, the wonder, the marvel, is that Julius achieved so much. He had great men working for him, and while there must have been in-fighting to secure what meagre resources were available, the tally of his works of patronage is formidable: the Stanze by Raphael, the Sistine Ceiling, the beginning of the reconstruction of St Peter's, which during his lifetime and Bramante's (who died in 1514) had reached little more than three of the great crossing piers. What must also be stressed is that when faced with the conflicts of interest and the rival demands on his limited resources it was the great public works that he completed, not his own tomb.

When Julius had Michelangelo virtually thrown out of the Vatican the artist hung around until April and then, recognizing defeat, flung back to Florence

44 ANDREA MANTEGNA
Entombment (engraving)

in a rage; riding by night he reached Poggibonsi in Florentine territory, where he was overtaken by messengers from the pope commanding him to return. He sent back word that he never would, because he did not deserve that his good and faithful service should be rewarded by being driven out like a rogue, and since His Holiness no longer wished to go on with the tomb, he was under no further obligation to him and did not wish to undertake any other obligations towards him. From Florence he wrote in May 1506 to Giuliano da Sangallo in Rome that the episode of the dismissal was not his only reason for leaving, and that he believed that if he had stayed it was his own tomb that would have been made before the pope's.

45 *Laocoön* Hellenistic original of *c.* 150 BC or later Roman copy

46 MICHELANGELO *Entombment c.* 1506

One work, however, does seem to have been begun during these Roman years, probably during the period when he was awaiting the arrival of the marble for the Julius Tomb and before he discovered that the pope did not intend to continue with the work. This is the unfinished *Entombment*. The picture has often been rejected as a work by Michelangelo, but it presents – in many ways like the *Manchester Madonna* – characteristics which make it very

46

difficult to assign it to any other artist. The figure of Christ is clearly
28 connected with the St Peter's *Pietà*, the group as a whole reflects Mantegna's
44 engraving of the *Entombment*, and the figure of the bearer on the left is
45 equally clearly influenced by the struggling *Laocoön*. Michelangelo had been present when the *Laocoön* was recognized by Giuliano da Sangallo in the marble group found by a peasant digging in a vineyard on the Esquiline on 14 January 1506, almost immediately after his return from Carrara. The group fascinated him, not only as one of the most famous antique statues described by Pliny the Elder and now brought to light, but as an example in antiquity of the expression of violent emotion and movement, and also of a profound spiritual struggle, since Laocoön and his sons are being killed by Apollo for having disobeyed him – they are the victims of divine wrath. It exercised a continuous influence on him, as one of the great works of antiquity which could be both an inspiration and an object of competition. In the Sistine Ceiling several of the *Ignudi*, and the dying *Haman* struggling on his cross, show the effects of the group; it reappears, though less directly perhaps, in the first pair of *Slaves* carved for the Julius Tomb, and the consciousness of it lingers on well into the *Last Judgment*.

The *Entombment* remained unfinished, possibly because of his abrupt return to Florence, though there is some internal evidence, in the stylistic changes between the group on the left and the two figures on the right, that he may have taken it up again briefly after the Sistine Ceiling was finished. The picture is painted entirely in oil-paint, and is the only such work he ever executed. Why it was started is more difficult to determine, but it has been suggested that the original form of the Julius Tomb, which enclosed a small chapel within the free-standing monument, may have called for a small altarpiece facing the sarcophagus of the pope. The abandonment of the free-standing project would have destroyed the motive for such a picture.

He resumed working on the commission for the Apostles, and also on the *Battle Cartoon*, but Julius, who now repented of his hastiness, tried by the intervention of friends to induce Michelangelo to return, since by May 1506 he had already decided that he wanted Michelangelo to decorate the vault of the Sistine Chapel. Bramante insinuated that Michelangelo might not be equal to the task, in that painting figures in sharp perspective was altogether different from doing them on the ground; nevertheless the pope now wrote to the Signoria of Florence in such terms that Soderini sent for Michelangelo and told him bluntly that 'he had had a passage of arms with the pope that even the King of France would not have dared to try, and since the Florentine state had no desire to go to war over him, he should no longer put them at risk but prepare to depart'. Michelangelo protested that he would sooner accept the offer from the Sultan to build a bridge between Pera and

Constantinople, but Soderini persuaded him to go to Bologna, where the pope had made his triumphant entry in November. Here took place the famous interview when a foolish bishop intervened to try to exculpate Michelangelo on the grounds that 'artisans did not know how to conduct themselves' and the pope drove out the offending bishop with blows, lest his artist, freshly affronted, should again depart in a rage of indignation. Julius commissioned the bronze statue of himself, three times life-size, which was placed over the main door of S. Petronio in Bologna, not with the book that Michelangelo suggested but with the sword that Julius insisted on, and with a raised key in the left hand and the right hand uplifted in blessing. The pope's gesture was so ambivalent that it was questionable whether he was blessing or menacing the people. After many difficulties over the casting the statue survived for only a short time, since when the Bentivogli retook the city in December 1511 it was pulled down and destroyed. Some idea of it can be obtained from Bandinelli's Louvre drawing for a monument to Clement VII, probably inspired by the Michelangelo, and many later statues of popes reflect the lost *Julius*. After completing the statue, Michelangelo returned to Florence and Julius returned to his warring campaign, but in April or early May 1508 the pope again summoned Michelangelo to Rome to undertake the painting of the Sistine Chapel Ceiling.

CHAPTER TWO

The Sistine Ceiling

The Sistine Chapel was built by the uncle of Julius II, Sixtus IV (Francesco della Rovere), who, immediately he became pope in 1471, began a building campaign to restore Rome after the decay and dilapidations of the long Avignon exile. Virtually nothing is known of preceding chapels on the site, except that one was restored by Martin V when he re-established the papacy in Rome in 1420, and Nicholas V, pope from 1447 to 1455, seems to have planned a *capella magna* large enough for papal ceremonies, but not to have begun it. Sixtus's new chapel was begun probably after 1475 and decorated between October 1481 and the spring of 1483: it was dedicated to the Virgin of the Assumption on 15 August 1483. Its size – about 132 ft by 45 ft (40·2 m by 13·6 m) – suggests that then, as now, it was to be the principal site for the Conclave, and this function is in fact central to the decoration of the chapel. *47* Originally, the plain, barn-like structure had windows all round: six on each long wall, and two on the short entrance and altar walls, but the two entrance-wall windows have always been blind and the two altar-wall windows were blocked up when Michelangelo's *Last Judgment* was painted. The original fresco decoration on the walls consisted of two typological series of the Life of Moses on the south or left-hand wall when facing the altar, and the Life of Christ on the north wall opposite. The altarpiece was an *Assumption of the Virgin*, now known only from a drawing from the Perugino studio (Vienna, Albertina), and it was flanked by the first pair of each series: the *Baptism of Christ* and the *Finding of Moses*. These frescoes were all destroyed to make room for the *Last Judgment*, as were the figures of Christ, flanked by Peter and Paul, which formed the central group from which the sequence of papal figures began. The ceiling itself is a shallow barrel-vault reaching down into pendentives between the spandrels over the windows, and in the corners, where pairs of spandrels meet, are larger triangular areas with curved tops. Above the windows are lunettes, and below the lunettes on either side of the windows the various artists who executed the frescoes of the Christ and Moses cycles also painted figures of the early popes. Between this area and the two fresco cycles there is a cornice carrying a passageway and a thin iron balustrade. The original ceiling decoration was a blue sky scattered about with golden stars – a common

47 Sistine Chapel, view of interior

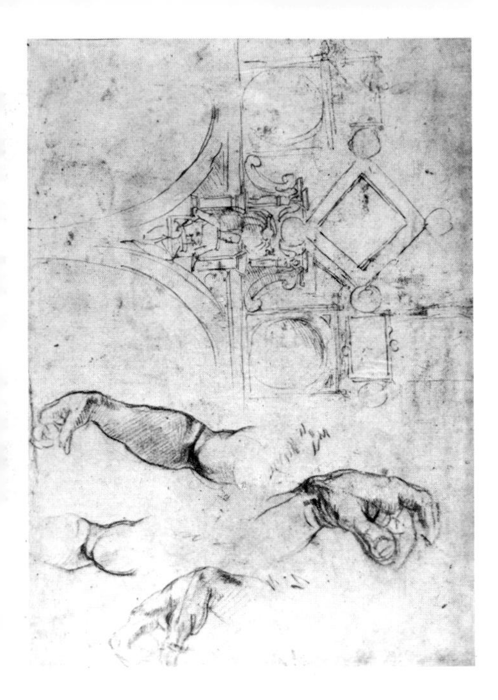

48 MICHELANGELO Sketch for decoration of the Sistine Ceiling 1508–09

Early Christian form of decoration for vaulting – and below the two fresco cycles were – and still are – painted curtains, over which eventually were hung on ceremonial occasions the tapestries for which Raphael made the cartoons.

The chapel was originally divided into two parts, a presbytery and an area for the congregation, by a screen which corresponded to the division in the superb inlaid marble floor and to the position of the choir balcony, but this screen was later moved to increase the size of the presbytery so that the half-way division which was important for the design of Michelangelo's Ceiling has been spoilt.

Julius's first idea for the Ceiling was a series of figures of the twelve Apostles enthroned, but the artist objected that it would be 'but a poor thing', and according to Michelangelo's own account the pope gave him a free hand to design it as he would. True to his normal practice, he does not mention anyone who might have assisted him with the planning of the content of the Ceiling, but the notion that he himself drew up the scheme of decoration from the iconographical standpoint may be dismissed. For all Condivi's claims that Michelangelo knew his Bible, and that Savonarola's sermons were an ever-living memory for him, ever since the Second Council of Nicaea in 787 it had been laid down that 'the churches were of the fathers who built them; only the art was of the artists', and the

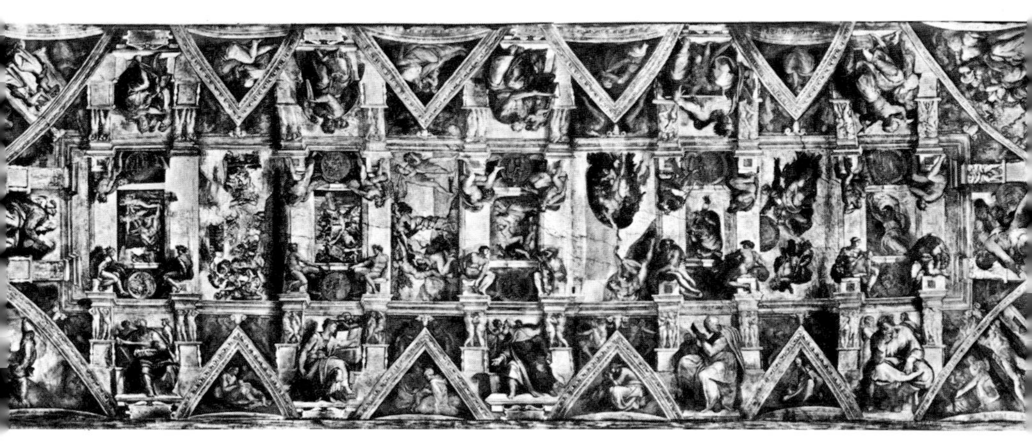

49 MICHELANGELO Sistine Ceiling 1508–12

iconographical content of the major chapel in the Vatican and the seat of the Conclave was not something which would have been left to a painter, however devout, however learned.

The interpretation of the various elements of the Ceiling has been attempted by almost every art historian who has been confronted with the problems the work presents. No complete interpretation has so far found favour with everyone; so many have been partly accepted and partly rejected that most suggestions court disaster of one kind or another, and the whole territory is filled with so many traps and pitfalls that it is only with extreme trepidation that a path is sought through this dangerous minefield. Nevertheless, the problems cannot be ignored or evaded despite their daunting difficulties. Perhaps a beginning may best be made by considering the decorations which Michelangelo found in the chapel when he started work. The two early fresco cycles form part of a known system of parallel examples: the Life of Moses as prophet and law-giver, as the saviour of his people in the Old Testament – the Judaic world *sub lege* – is contrasted with the Life of Christ as saviour and redeemer in the New Testament – the Christian world *sub gratia*. The row of imaginary portraits of early popes stresses the Apostolic Succession from Christ and Peter in the fresco of the *Charge to Peter* – the *Giving of the Keys* – reminding the electors at a Conclave that their duty is to elect a successor to Peter himself. This existing arrangement meant that while Julius's first thought of an Apostle series would not have been totally out of keeping, it would, as Michelangelo objected, have been a poor solution and a thin, if not banal, programme,

49, 62

particularly as the huge area would have meant that a large part of the Ceiling would have been covered with purely decorative architectural elements as a framework for the enthroned Apostle figures. The decision was taken to work out a scheme earlier than the Moses cycle and to represent the world *ante legem* from the first day of Creation to man's degradation in sin which made both the Law and Salvation necessary. To this was to be joined a series of prophets and sibyls, as bringers of the word to Jew and Gentile, and four great examples of Divine intervention for the salvation of the Jews – the salvation, that is, of the Law and the House of David from which the Saviour would eventually arise. Who worked out the scheme is unknown; no programme has survived, but it has been suggested that two major theologians were concerned: Egidius of Viterbo, Prior-General of the Augustinians and Julius's favourite preacher, who was a luminary of classical as well as Biblical learning, and Santi Pagnini, at one time Prior of S. Marco in Florence and a disciple of Savonarola, and a famous Biblical scholar.

Two tiny drawings survive to indicate the first Apostle scheme (London, *48* British Museum; Detroit, Institute of Arts). Both show a compartmented area with an indication of architectural elements, cut up into small frames supported by figures presumably of angels, since they are shown winged, although Michelangelo deliberately avoided winged figures (the only *15* known cases, both very early, are the *Angel bearing a Candlestick* and a tiny *40* tentative feathering of one shoulder of a figure in the *Manchester Madonna*). In the Ceiling the architectural framework is of major importance, since it provides the links between the parts, and both unifies and separates them. It also stresses the flatter central part of the barrel-vault, and by its long bold horizontals helps to isolate the ceiling proper from the strongly framed spandrels which impinge upon it. Within the long central area are nine narrative panels or 'histories', four large ones stretching the whole way across from one framing cornice to the other, and five smaller ones, each flanked by four of the nude male figures of athletes – the *Ignudi* – who between them support garlands and shields: these smaller panels surmount the figures of the enthroned prophets and sibyls who alternate on the pendentives. At either end is an enthroned prophet, who closes the composition: Zechariah over the entrance doorway, and Jonah over the altar.

The choice of the seven prophets is curious: four are major prophets – Isaiah, Jeremiah, Daniel and Ezekiel – and three are minor ones – Zechariah, *55* Joel and Jonah. Zechariah over the door is a prophet of gloom, of punishment for the backslidings of the Jews, but he also prophesies the establishment of the Kingdom, the building of a new Jerusalem and a new Temple, the restoration of peace, justice and prosperity, and the destruction

50 MICHELANGELO *Ezekiel*

51 MICHELANGELO *Joel*

52 MICHELANGELO *Isaiah*

of the enemies of Zion. He is one of the prophets of Christ's Passion, for he speaks of the entry into Jerusalem 'of the King of salvation, lowly and riding upon an ass', of the thirty pieces of silver, and of the wounds piercing Christ's *51* hands. Joel is a prophet of disaster, of the laying waste of the land, of the need for repentance and the blessings which flow from it, full of dire threats of vengeance pursuing sin. He speaks of the defeat of the Assyrians – the army from the North – and his gentlest words are those marvellous ones, 'your old men shall dream dreams, your young men shall see visions'. In Joel the only overt references to a Redeemer are mentions of a 'teacher unto justice', but the prophet has the distinction that Peter, in his Pentecostal sermon (Acts 2, 17–21), quotes Joel 2, 28–32 as fulfilled in the miraculous gift of tongues, and by association, therefore, Joel is acknowledged as the prophet of the Holy Spirit. Yet is he an angry prophet.

50 Ezekiel's book begins with his awesome vision of the four beasts which become personified later as the emblems of the Evangelists. He denounces the defilers of the sanctuary, predicts famine, war, pestilence, destruction,

53 MICHELANGELO *Daniel*

54 MICHELANGELO *Jeremiah*

and the most fearful punishments for the sins of Jerusalem. Occasionally he softens to promise God's pity for his people, and his only reference to Christ's mission is an oblique reference to the Shepherd guiding, leading, feeding his flock. He too is an angry, violent prophet since he is the prophet of the Babylonian Exile which he suffered, using his gift of prophecy to exhort his fellow deportees to repent of their sins and to return to the worship of the one God. Isaiah is the major prophet of the Redemption: 52 fierce and denunciatory, with promises of deliverance from the Assyrian alternating with cries of woe against sinners and idolaters. Then comes the tender hymn of 'unto us a child is born, unto us a son is given', with the promise of the Virgin birth, the Tree of Jesse, the lion and the lamb lying down together, and the tragic foretelling of the Man despised and rejected, the Man of Sorrows, wounded for our transgressions, brought as a lamb to the slaughter. Isaiah storms and rages at the iniquities and idolatries before him, but he weeps too in bitter suffering and travail of spirit. Jeremiah weeps 54 more tragically, since it fell to him to predict the destruction of Jerusalem to a

55 MICHELANGELO *Zechariah*

people who refused to believe him, who rejected his counsels of submission to the Assyrians which might have saved them from total annihilation, so that he prefigures Christ weeping over the destruction of the city. But his despair and his sufferings are not relieved by any vision of Redemption, only by his faith that the Kingdom would eventually be restored.

53 Daniel is not only a prophet, but the exemplar of the righteous man, the wise and trusted counsellor, the just viceroy, persecuted for obedience to the

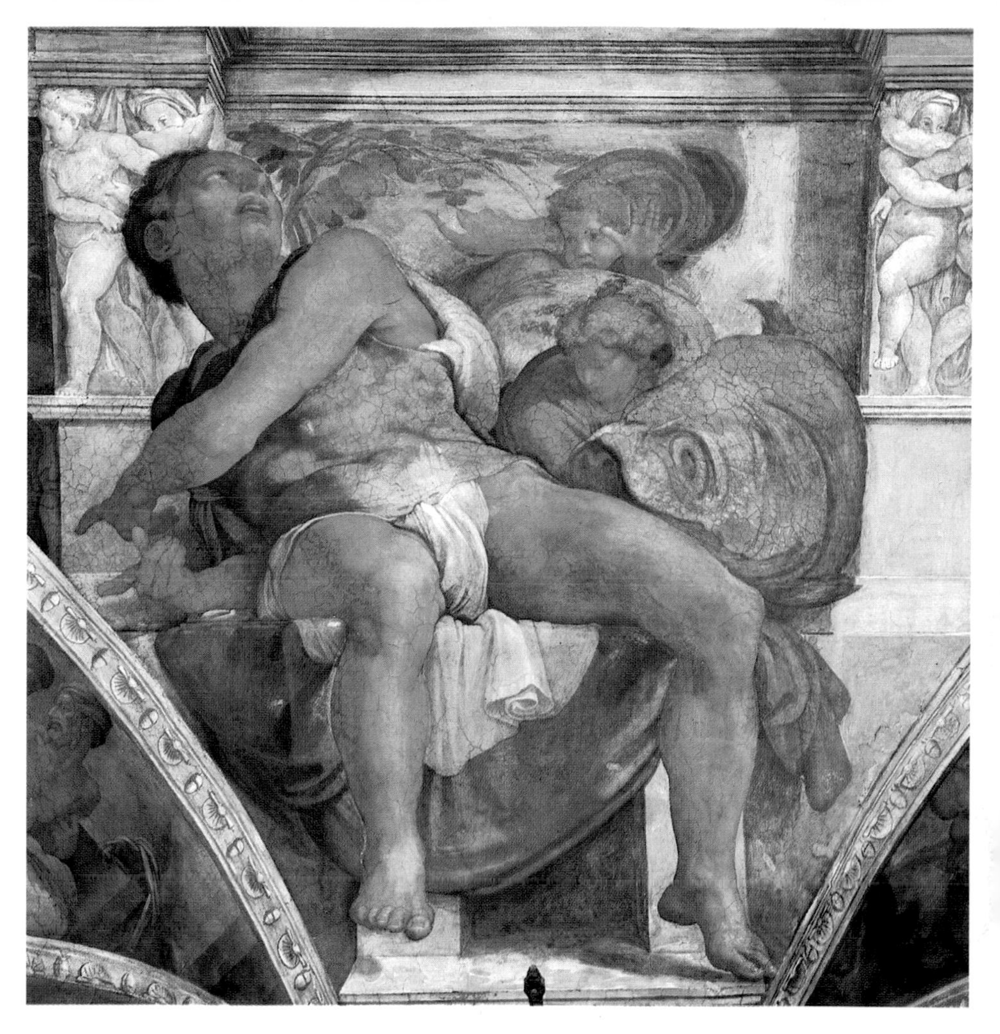

56 MICHELANGELO *Jonah*

Law and vindicated by the mercy of God. He is the enlightened man of learning, the expounder of dreams, and he figures among the prophets through his actions as much as through his words, which constantly express the belief that God will preserve the faithful, and will restore His Kingdom upon earth. His is the faith that never wavers, as great as Jeremiah's but far less tragic. Jonah's prophetic role is minimal. When the word of God came to him bidding him prophesy to the people of Nineveh he fled in terror from

56

57 MICHELANGELO *Delphic Sibyl*

58 (*right*) MICHELANGELO *Erythraean Sibyl*

59 (*far right*) MICHELANGELO *Persian Sibyl*

the mission, but found that flight was useless. He is unconsciously the precursor of Christ in that the death to which he was thrown was accepted by him willingly as a means of saving the ship and the sailors; his three days in the belly of the whale prefigure the Entombment, and his being cast up by the whale is a figure of the Resurrection. But Jonah is an unwilling, rebellious prophet, not only appalled at the mission God forces him to perform, but angry and reproachful to God because after he has suffered so much in order to obey, God then spares the repentant city instead of destroying it. His place over the altar is neither for his virtues nor for his mission, but for his unique prefiguration, for he turns to look at God above him while pointing to the figure of Christ which once stood on the wall below.

The sibyls are the time-honoured representatives of ancient non-Jewish prophecy, and are female figures because in the ancient world the mantic powers were held to be peculiarly a gift of women. No ancient sibylline books survived, but apocryphal prophecies attributed to the sibyls made it simple, natural even, to include them so as to justify a Gentile, as against a purely Jewish, tradition of prophetic utterance. Their cryptic utterances were all concerned with the coming of Christ: the Cumaean sibyl, in Virgil's

61

Fourth Eclogue, foretells the Virgin birth of the Redeemer; in the *City of God*, St Augustine devotes a chapter to the Erythraean sibyl who is said to have foretold the Last Judgment, and she is included in the *Dies Irae* in the words 'teste David cum Sibylla'; the Persian sibyl was credited with a long prophecy referring to the Virgin's triumph over the Beast of the Apocalypse; the Libyan sibyl prophesies the coming of the day when that which is hidden shall be revealed and the Queen shall hold the King in her lap; and the Delphic sibyl proclaims that a prophet shall be born of a Virgin knowing no human corruption. The five sibyls chosen for the Ceiling from the ten (later twelve) available were the recognized major sibyls, and double as the representatives of ancient civilizations: Delphica for Greece; Persica for the ancient Persian Empire; Erythraea – who also had a legendary Biblical connection as Noah's daughter-in-law – for Ionia, on the Lidyan coast of what is now Turkey; Libyca for the African continent; and finally Cumaea, the Roman sibyl.

58

59

60

57

All the prophets and sibyls, except Daniel, are accompanied by two small figures which hover in the background and echo in some measure the major figure they stand behind. These expressive little genii are probably derived

60 MICHELANGELO *Libyan Sibyl*

from Pico della Mirandola's thesis that everyone is accompanied throughout his life by spirits or angels reflecting aspects of his nature. One of these little genii stands for his spiritual nature, the other for his corporal nature. Usually one of them dominates the other and reflects the mood or character of the prophet or sibyl more powerfully. The exception, Daniel, has only one genius, standing between his legs and supporting the weight of his book like a tiny Atlas, though it is possible that the other figure once appeared in the

53

61 MICHELANGELO *Cumaean Sibyl*

faint smudge behind the prophet's massive left arm where there appears to be an area of damage. Beside each prophet and sibyl and surmounting the side supports of their thrones are two small caryatid *putti*, male and female. Each throne has different pairs, but each pair is drawn from the same cartoon reversed, with only a change in the direction of the lighting on the limbs.

Below the thrones on the long walls, holding up the name-tablets of the prophets and sibyls, are ten more *putti*, the six early ones in pairs on reversed cartoons, the four later ones all different, as if Michelangelo found it easier to paint them freehand than to bother with tracing a cartoon. Further almost obliterated bronze-coloured figures lie crouched or twisted in deep shadow in the triangular spaces between the outside of the thrones and the pointed tops of the spandrels; again they are based in pairs on reversed cartoons, differentiated only by the light falling on them. Various interpretations have been placed on these pairs of figures and on the *putti* of the tablets, and the most acceptable (Tolnay's) is that they are not merely decorative but are figurations of the genii which characterize mankind: the spirits of good and evil, of divine, human and animal impulses. These ideas would be perfectly consonant with the whole tenor of Michelangelo's basically Neoplatonic thought, and would be in no way out of place in the religious scheme of the Ceiling.

If the prophets and sibyls are considered in relation to the earlier decoration, it will be seen that the Life of Christ sequence is surmounted by three sibyls who proclaim in various forms the Virgin birth and the coming of Christ, while Isaiah is also the prophet of Christ's coming, and Daniel the unwavering believer in the establishment of God's Kingdom. The Moses sequence is surmounted by two sibyls who predict the Apocalypse and the Last Judgment, and by three prophets of disaster: Jeremiah and Ezekiel, prophets of the destruction of Jerusalem and the dispersal of the Jews, and Joel, whose promise that the Assyrians will eventually be defeated implies the miseries and sufferings which preceded that event. If then the individual figures of prophets and sibyls are considered in relation to their roles and their words, it will immediately be seen that these do not completely agree. *54, 52* Jeremiah is sunk in profound gloom; Isaiah listens abstractedly to the voices *50* he hears within him; Ezekiel turns with angry energy, his outstretched hand – 'Thus saith the Lord God, Smite with thy hand' – in furious expostulation and his other grasping the roll which God thrust into his mouth and bade *56* him eat; Jonah writhes convulsively between the Two Persons of the Godhead: but for an interpretation of Zechariah, Joel and Daniel their prophecies and their personalities do not help at all. It can be argued that Isaiah and Daniel are personifications of the Contemplative and the Active Life, but what then of the other prophets? Edgar Wind put forward the very persuasive argument that they are to be seen as personifications of the Seven Gifts of the Holy Spirit which Isaiah defines in 11, 1–3: Wisdom, Understanding, Counsel, Fortitude, Knowledge, Compassion, and the Fear of the Lord (in the Authorized Version Compassion is omitted; the Vulgate lists all seven gifts). This would involve looking at the figures Michelangelo has created from two separate standpoints: that of their prophetic missions and that of an abstract quality imposed on each figure from without.

Zechariah, thumbing through the pages of his book as if seeking the right *55* passage, would fit well with Wisdom, just as his prophecies of the restoration of the Kingdom and the rebuilding of Jerusalem and the Temple can be fitted to Julius's own projects for his temporal power. Joel, calm, with an inquiring *51* and thoughtful expression, his high-domed forehead and frown expressive of intellectual concentration, fits better with the concept of Understanding than with the tenor of his own prophecies; Isaiah, reflective and troubled, *52* accords with the concept of Counsel or Deliberation. There is no difficulty in equating Ezekiel with Might or Fortitude, and because of Julius's loathing *50* for his Borgia predecessor, Ezekiel may have been included deliberately in this meeting-place of the Conclave because of his awesome predictions of the punishments of those who defile the sanctuary. The decisive Daniel can *53* easily be equated with Knowledge, the dejected Jeremiah with Compassion, *54* and the affrighted Jonah with the Fear of the Lord. *56*

Once it is accepted that various levels of meaning may coexist, then certain, though few, topical references are admissible. The sibyls present a different problem, and here there is no compelling need to drive the analogies further than the equation of the sibyls with their geographical links and the tenor of their apocryphal prophecies, with perhaps an extension into the different types of womanhood they present: Delphica, the youthful *57* visionary, filled with an utterance which surges from her without her understanding what she says – the personification of the Divine afflatus and possession by the spirit of the god; Cumaea, massive and vigorous in her old *61* age; Libyca, filled with youthful energy and decisiveness; Erythraea, calm, *60, 58* considered, thoughtful, intent upon her text; Persica, aged and feeble, *59* peering short-sightedly at her book, as if incredulous of what she finds there. Wind argues that the sibyls personify Paul's five Gifts of the Spirit (1 Cor. 14, 26), which were expounded by St Thomas Aquinas and paraphrased by Erasmus: Psalm or mystical utterance, Doctrine or moral instruction, Tongue or the gift of the word, Exposition to make the word clear, Revelation to explain meaning. This is an attractive theory, but does nothing to suggest other than very subjectively which gift should be attached to which figure. The same objection of a purely subjective interpretation may be levelled at the equation of the prophets with Isaiah's Gifts of the Spirit, or at the Neoplatonic interpretation of the genii, the caryatid *putti*, the crouching figures in the triangles beside the thrones, and the animal-like *putti* who hold the tablets. The words of St Thomas Aquinas must be remembered, however: 'For one thing may have similitude to many; for which reason it is impossible to proceed from any thing mentioned in Scripture to an unambiguous meaning.' One of the major difficulties with the Sistine Ceiling is that if one part is significant, then all parts are.

Moreover, if all subjective interpretation is ruled out, then no interpretation but a superficially material one is possible, which, in view of the nature and location of the work, is equally unbelievable.

The central area of the Ceiling is taken up by the nine narrative panels of the 'histories'. These begin over the altar, although Michelangelo in executing the work began over the entrance door, and because of certain problems and changes in the execution it is perhaps more satisfactory to proceed as Michelangelo himself did.

The contract was signed on 10 May 1508, stipulating a fee of 3,000 ducats, with an advance of 500 ducats, but almost immediately another contract, doubling the fee, was made which clearly reflects the change from the original project with the Apostles only, to the new project with the 'histories'. A scaffolding was erected by 27 July 1508, which gives just over two months for the working out of the programme and the artist's preparatory work. The scaffolding extended from the door to half way along the chapel – that is, as far as the screen which then divided the chapel in two, and marked the division between the clergy and the laity. This first part was apparently painted between August 1508 and August 1510, and consists of the three 'histories' of Noah, the *Fall and Expulsion* and the *Creation of Eve*, together with four of the prophets and two of the sibyls corresponding to them, and the spandrels which accompany them, but not the lunettes. If the Ceiling is looked at in perspective from one end of the chapel the conclusion that the spandrels were painted at the same time as the vault and the pendentives is inevitable. The lunettes were certainly painted last, probably from a movable scaffolding which projected from the passage under the windows, but from such a scaffolding it would be difficult to reach up into the area of the spandrels. Moreover, the spandrels exhibit changes similar to those appearing in the main part of the Ceiling.

The 'histories' in the first part begin with the story of Noah: the *Deluge*, the *Sacrifice of Noah* and his family after their deliverance, and the *Drunkenness of Noah*. It seems fairly certain from internal evidence that the *Deluge* was painted first. It is displaced in sequence since, being a very large scene, Michelangelo placed it in the middle of the three scenes, using the two smaller fields for the other two scenes which contain fewer figures. In some ways the *Deluge* goes back to the *Battle of Cascina*, in that it is a large composition almost entirely of nude figures, depicting desperate attempts to escape from the rising waters. Men and women, some carrying their children, climb hills, take refuge on rocks, shelter under makeshift canopies, struggle to keep invaders from a fragile boat by beating off those who try to climb in, clamber fighting on to the substructure of the Ark itself, push before them their pitiful household goods, or, overwhelmed by the disaster,

63

62 MICHELANGELO Sistine Ceiling (detail)

63 Michelangelo *The Deluge*

lie apathetically staring before them. One man bears the body of a drowned son, another climbs a tree, and in the background the dove flutters from the Ark and Noah invokes God's protection. The figures straggle in a long disorganized skein over the picture space, diffused in action and small in scale compared to the size of the field. Technical analysis confirms that the actual *intonaco* of the fresco surface is rougher than the rest of the Ceiling, though this type of argument is difficult in view of the damage the fresco has

64 Michelangelo *The Sacrifice of Noah*

sustained (an explosion of a powder-magazine in the Castel S. Angelo in 1797 caused part of the Ceiling to fall).

Both the *Drunkenness of Noah* and the *Sacrifice* show a clear change of scale in the figures; this suggests that after completing the *Deluge* Michelangelo took steps to examine his work from the floor of the chapel and decided that the scale of his figures was not large enough. It has been argued that the *Sacrifice* was painted before the *Drunkenness*, but this is not reasonable. Firstly, the Delphic sibyl looks back to the Madonna of the *Doni Tondo* and even to the Madonna of the *Pitti Tondo* in her pose and in the rounded frontality of the forms; secondly, the four nude figures of athletes – the *Ignudi* – who are seated on the small pedestals round the *Drunkenness of Noah* are based on reversed cartoons of the same figure in each pair (there are very slight differences but not enough to count seriously), and the differentiation between each figure in a pair is achieved purely by the treatment of the light falling on them. After this initial pairing of the figures Michelangelo abandoned the idea, and the rest of the *Ignudi* are all different. It is not sensible to argue that having started by making them all different he would then have reverted to the older system of reversed cartoons. (As a result of the 1797 explosion, one of the figures was lost, but it is known from an engraving.) It is true that the scene of Noah's degradation has larger figures than the *Sacrifice*, but the scene called for fewer figures and for a less congested composition. Moreover, the figures in the earliest pair of spandrels are also in tightly knit groups, and there is a clearly discernible change of

65, 64

39

38

77

65 MICHELANGELO *The Drunkenness of Noah*

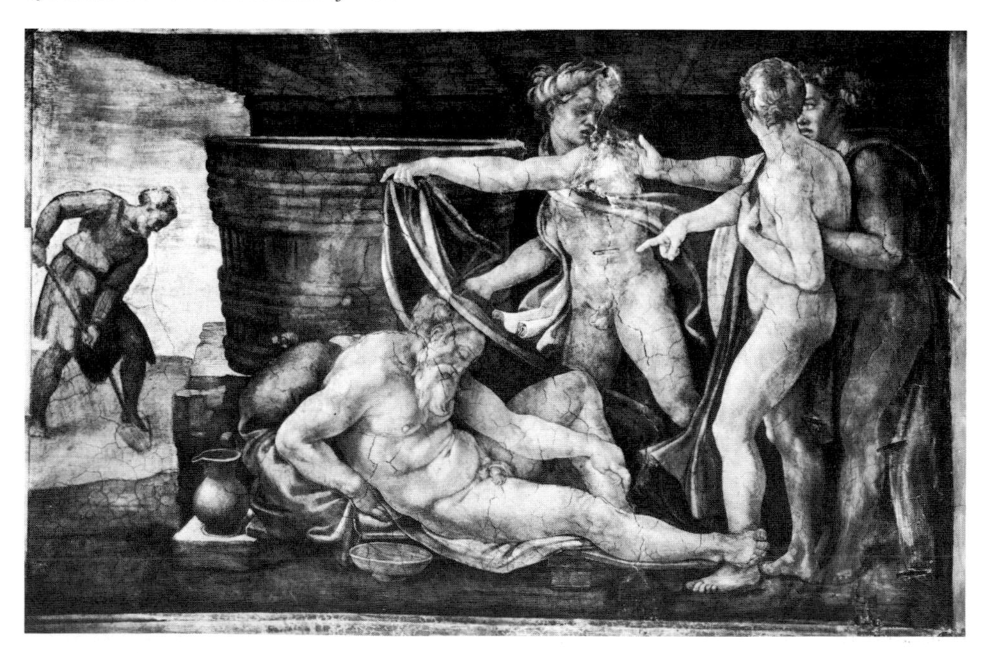

scale between Delphica and her neighbour Isaiah, and also between Joel and Erythraea, for the level of Isaiah's plinth is lowered, and Erythraea fills the space in which she sits more fully than Joel does. It would, however, be perfectly reasonable that after completing these three 'histories' and their attendant figures, Michelangelo then painted Zechariah over the door – the figure is bulkier, the head and hands larger, and the space in which the prophet sits much wider – and the two corner spandrels, where the group of *David and Goliath* is simpler, larger, less diffused than the more complex story of *Judith and Holofernes* on the opposite side. The three Noah narratives and the accompanying figures were probably completed by 3 June 1509, since Albertini in his *Opusculum de mirabilibus urbis Romae*, published in 1510, mentions at that date seeing 'beautiful paintings on the ceiling by the Florentine Michelangelo'.

72

73

The next two narratives before the half-way division of the chapel are the *Fall and Expulsion*, treated as one continuous scene, and the *Creation of Eve*. The device of continuous representation – that is, the depiction of consecutive incidents within the same frame – was by now very old-fashioned, but Michelangelo uses the device because there was no way of fitting all his narratives into separate fields. It is clear from the way in which Michelangelo treats his figures that though Eve is the one tempted, the lusty Adam does not refuse participation in the first sin, and his eager gesture and Eve's voluptuous pose contrast pitifully with the anguished recognition of

66

66 MICHELANGELO *The Fall and Expulsion*

67 MICHELANGELO *The Creation of Eve*

the consequences of their trespass. Even in the Garden of Eden no hint of Paradise appears – just a few rocks and a tree almost as naked as the one in the *Deluge* – while the empty world into which the pair are driven by the angel is bleak and inhospitable. One interesting and striking point is that Michelangelo has made the serpent a female figure. In the *Creation of Eve* the Godhead appears for the first time. He is a brooding and unwilling Creator, aware in the moment of calling the first woman into being of what will be the consequences of the act. He bids her arise and she stumbles forward, half-wondering, half-cringing, while the unconscious Adam slumps in the abandon not so much of sleep as of the night of the soul. All the figures are now large enough to fill the field entirely, and that of God would burst the confines of the frame were He to stand upright instead of leaning forward in the gesture of summons.

67

At this point – probably September 1510 – the work stopped. There is some argument about how long it stopped; Michelangelo travelled to Bologna twice to try to get the pope to provide money for moving and

68 MICHELANGELO *The Creation of Adam*

rebuilding the scaffolding and also to pay something for his own sustenance, money which Julius was in no position to provide, since at this time he was in the thick of the bitter campaign against Ferrara and Mirandola, and was journeying backwards and forwards from the battle-ground to Bologna, which he eventually lost in May 1511. Julius did not return to Rome until June 1511, and then threw himself into the organization of the Lateran Council with such tireless energy that in July he became seriously ill so that a Conclave was expected, although his iron constitution was such that he recovered by the end of the month. Work on the Ceiling certainly began again by February 1511, since some money for the scaffolding was provided in January 1511, and Michelangelo complained that he might have to go to Bologna again in February to secure more. It would appear, therefore, that the last part of the central portion, plus the prophets and sibyls and the spandrels, was executed between February and August 1511. This left only the lunettes, and these were completed by the autumn of 1512, since the whole Ceiling was uncovered by the Vigil of All Saints (31 October) when Julius and the court inspected the work, the chapel being reopened for services on 1 November. Michelangelo's only comment was in a letter to his father written in early October 1512, in which he remarks: 'I have finished the chapel which I was painting: the pope is very satisfied: and the other matters are not turning out as I wished; but these times are very unfavourable to our art . . .'

The remaining part of the Ceiling over the presbytery consists of four narrative panels, all concerned with the major acts of the Creation: the

Creation of Adam, *God separating Earth from Water*, the *Creation of the Sun, Moon and Stars and the Creation of Vegetation* and *God separating Light from Darkness*. In the *Creation of Adam* – or rather the Creation of Man – God leans forward from the encircling swathe of drapery and from the support of the angels who bear Him to reach forward in the marvellous gesture of life-giving energy to the almost inert figure of Man lying on the barren hillside, so that his frame is suddenly endowed with life and movement. It is a large group, simple in its conception, total in its rendering of the act of creation. Under God's left arm the figure of a woman shelters: the as yet uncreated Eve, surprised at the sight of her coming destiny in the Man lying before her, and unconscious still of the fate she will bring upon him. The three scenes that follow are concerned entirely with the work of the Godhead in the creation of the Universe: benignly omnipotent in the separating of land and water; furiously active in a huge swirling movement as He creates the firmament and earth's vegetation; swinging from one side of the picture space to the other in a great arc as He turns like a curving projectile and hurtles on His course; and then as a vast presence more than a concrete figure surging against the ragged clouds and cleaving the light from the dark. It is

68

69–71

69 MICHELANGELO *God separating Earth from Water*

70 MICHELANGELO *The Creation of the Sun, Moon and Stars*

from this apocalyptic vision that the terrified Jonah thrusts himself away as he leans down to point to the figure of Christ below.

From the point of division between the two halves of the Ceiling, after Michelangelo had been able to see the effect of the first part of his work when the scaffolding was moved forward, the whole scale and effect of the work changed. The Cumaean sibyl was the first to show the total change of scale, which had already begun to affect the earlier prophets and sibyls attached to the first narratives. Michelangelo lowered the base of the thrones on which the later prophets and sibyls sit even more than he had done already so as to give more room for their enlarged proportions, although at no point did he disturb the line of the architectural cornice above their heads. Also, while Cumaea, Daniel and Libyca are considerably larger than Delphica and Isaiah, whom they accompany on the north wall, only Persica and Jeremiah on the south wall share their new proportions: Ezekiel is given slightly less space than Erythraea. In the spandrels the same features are found: the groups are simpler, the figures larger, bulkier, fewer, and in the double spandrels at the end of the chapel above the altar the space is filled with figures in urgent movement and violently contorted gestures. The four double spandrels should be considered together, since they represent yet another theme in the scheme of the Ceiling. They treat of the four great episodes of salvation in the history of the Jews: the successful combat between David and Goliath

72–75

71 MICHELANGELO *God separating Light from Darkness*

72 MICHELANGELO *David and Goliath*

and the deliverance from the Philistines; the saga of Judith, who saved the children of Israel from destruction by Holofernes, captain of the besieging Assyrians; the story of Esther, who by courage and guile saved her people from destruction by Haman, the chief minister of Ahasuerus; the salvation of the Israelites, who, rebelling against Moses, brought upon themselves the plague of fiery serpents and were only saved by gazing at the brazen serpent set up among them – a prefiguration of the Crucifixion. The first pair of spandrels are relatively simple: David straddles the gigantic form of his fallen foe, while from the shadows affrighted soldiers look on; Judith turns to look back at the body of the man she has killed, lying sprawled on the bed, while throwing a cloth over the terrible burden her maid lifts up on to her head. The second pair are more complex. The device of continuous representation is again employed in the Esther story, so that on one side the sleepless king is having the records read to him and hearing of his preservation by Mordecai from the murderous chamberlains; in the centre Mordecai sits at the king's

72

73

74

73 MICHELANGELO *Judith and Holofernes*

gate, while Haman is bidden to honour him; on the left Esther sits at the banquet with the king and Haman, whom she denounces; and in the centre again Haman is crucified upon the gallows he had prepared for Mordecai. The striking figure of Haman is obviously derived from the *Laocoön*, which had been discovered in 1506, and which had already been influential in Michelangelo's art. The scene with the brazen serpent is a confused mass of figures, presaging in the treatment of two groups – one of the believers who gaze upon the symbol of salvation, and the other of those who, writhing in agony and death, turn their backs upon it – the division of mankind into the saved and the damned: a prefiguration of the Last Judgment. As in the other scenes in the later part of the Ceiling, the scale of the figures and their complexity has increased until the field is barely large enough to contain all that the artist has endeavoured to cram into it.

45

75

There is also a distinct change in colour, and in the treatment of the decorative details. In the earlier parts of the Ceiling, the colour is more

74 MICHELANGELO *Esther and Haman*

descriptive and much brighter and paler. The prophets wear dress of variegated colours, the sibyls' robes are often of shot colours, and the shields picked out in gold add brightness to the whole. In the later parts the whole treatment of colour is more sober. There is no gold – which Michelangelo realized was a waste of effort in view of the distance at which the scenes had to be viewed, and also because it merely imparted an old-fashioned look to decorate such scenes with superfluous ornament. The larger size of the figures, the concentration upon the massive forms of the Godhead, and the stronger effects of light and shade used in the *Ignudi*, enable Michelangelo to simplify the colour scheme so that effects of light and shadow rather than colour are what strike the eye. There is also a steady progression in the *chiaroscuro*, not only in the stronger contrasts between the first and the second parts of the Ceiling, but also in the difference between the north and the south sides. Where Michelangelo experimented with changes of scale, he did so first on the north wall, where the better light from the windows opposite

75 MICHELANGELO *The Brazen Serpent*

made it easier for him to see what he was doing. In the lunettes, however, the colours are almost uniformly dark, kept so deliberately for expressive reasons.

One of the great problems of the narrative panels is the meaning of the *Ignudi*, the nude male figures which are seated on the pedestals at the corners of the smaller 'histories'. They display every kind of movement from lassitude to the most violent contortion; they embody every feeling from apathy to joy and struggle. They have been variously interpreted as the Platonic personifications of Beauty and Goodness, as the joyous spirits of an age before the Fall, as the emblems of life and movement, but whatever meaning may be thrust upon them they have at least three practical functions. They serve to mask the changes of scale between the figures on the pendentives and those within the narrative panels by inserting a further scale between the parts at the top of the Ceiling and those on the lowest part of the curve. Seated on their small blocks, they are posed in such a way that

69, 77

76 Michelangelo *Ancestors of Christ: Abiud and Eliachim*

77 Michelangelo First pair of *Ignudi* with part of *The Drunkenness of Noah*

78 MICHELANGELO *Ancestors of Christ: Manasses and Amon*

their legs conceal the change of perspective between the central architectural framework and the slight perspective of the thrones themselves. They also stress by their frontality the rejection of any illusionistic perspective system on the central part of the vault. Here Michelangelo has deliberately avoided the pitfalls of the *sotto in sù* type of illusionism which was now creeping into ceiling-painting, following the examples of Mantegna in Mantua and Melozzo da Forlì in Rome, and has avoided in every way possible foreshortenings of the figures which would have created the illusion of separate windows into space above the spectator's head. The other function of the *Ignudi* is that, placed on the architectural framework between the 'histories', and even impinging on them in some instances, they serve as *repoussoirs*, and by pushing the narratives back behind the framework they unify the panels and stress their continuity in a different order of space. The 'histories' themselves are conceived as existing in an ideal space behind the architectural frame, since the sky within them is continuous, beginning over Zechariah and ending over Jonah as a plain blue element.

The *Ignudi*, who strain at holding garlands or draperies between them, support small medallions painted in bronze and, in the earliest ones, picked out in gold, depicting scenes from the Books of Kings and Chronicles,

79 MICHELANGELO Study for the *Libyan Sibyl*

chiefly of the killings of bad kings and the vengeances of Old Testament warriors. These scenes link in a rather allusive way the time zones of the Ceiling, for the central part of the Ceiling is concerned with the world *ante legem*, while the medallions depict incidents from the violent world of the Old Testament, and the prophets and sibyls belong to the era of Mosaic Law and look forward by their prophecies to the world *sub gratia*. The four double spandrels at the corners depict the operation of God's mercy for the preservation of the Jews, while the smaller spandrels contain figures from the genealogy of Christ, linking the world of the Ceiling narratives to the world below. In the lunettes these Ancestors of Christ are depicted in a long series of depressed, oppressed, crushed figures representing humanity at its lowest ebb: the people who wait in darkness for the coming of the new dawn, who in their postures and expressions characterize the 'hope long deferred that maketh the heart sick', but who were never to know that 'when the day cometh it is as the dawn of life'.

76, 78

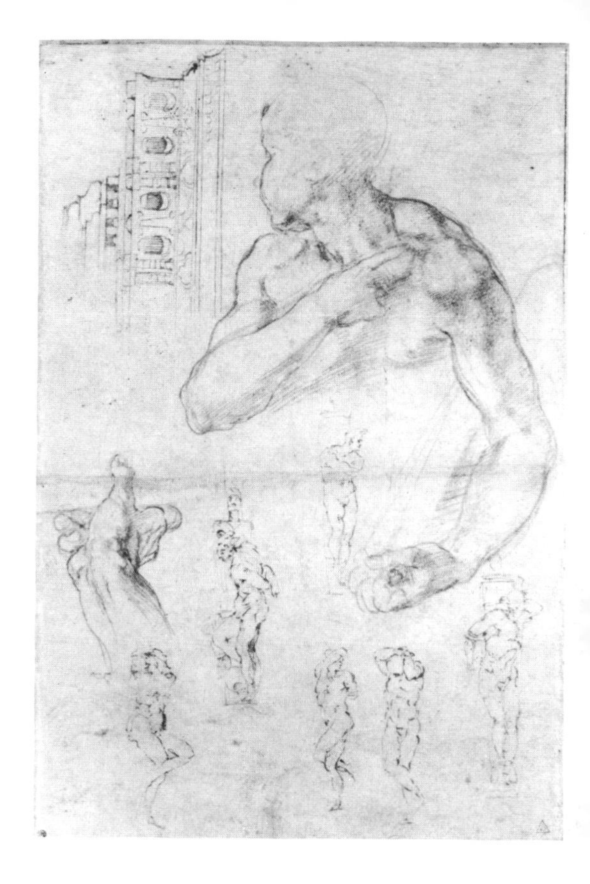

80 MICHELANGELO Study for a *putto* and for the right hand of the *Libyan Sibyl*, with sketches for the Julius Tomb

The sweep of the Ceiling is one of the supreme triumphs of genius. From the altar, as the spectator turns to look down the length of the chapel, the cycle of Creation unfolds, from the immense majesty of the creating Godhead to His supreme creation of Man in His own image, endowed with the immortality of His own life force. Then, at the point of junction between the presbytery and the world, comes the creation of Eve, shuddering from the side of the unconscious Adam to a life which enables Sin and Punishment to enter the world, to set it on the path which leads to the Divine anger of the Deluge and the survival of the tiny nucleus which has escaped the general degradation, but which itself immediately falls into Sin, and in the drunkenness of Noah and the mockery of his impious sons completes the tragedy of the degeneration of mankind. Against the tragic prophecies are set only the promises of redemption of a few lone voices, and the fervent belief in the regeneration of mankind through the sinlessness of one woman who will, a second Eve, bring salvation through a second Adam.

CHAPTER THREE

Rome and Florence, 1513–34
The Julius Tomb. The San Lorenzo Façade.
The Medici Chapel. The Biblioteca Laurenziana

In his *Life of Michelangelo*, Condivi described the history of the Julius Tomb as the 'Tragedy of the Tomb', and its difficulties and disappointments pursued Michelangelo for forty years. He must have restarted work on it soon after finishing the Sistine Ceiling, for there is an angry letter dating from the autumn of 1512 demanding from one Baldassare, who was probably an agent, what had become of the marble that had been paid for, and another written in November to his father says laconically, 'I am well, thank God, and working.' The inference that it was on designs for the Tomb may be made from a drawing for the Libyan sibyl which has, on the lower part of the sheet (Michelangelo never wasted paper), a number of little sketches for the *Slaves* projected for the lower part of the monument. *80*

The situation altered radically with the death of Julius in February 1513. The pope had charged two cardinals, Lorenzo Pucci and Leonardo Grosso della Rovere, the nephew of Sixtus IV, to see that his tomb was completed, and he had left 10,000 ducats for the purpose. Leo X was elected on 11 March 1513; he was the Cardinal Giovanni de' Medici, Lorenzo the Magnificent's son, whom Michelangelo had known in his youthful years when he had lived in the Medici household. Leo showed no inclination to employ Michelangelo; clearly Raphael's art and personality were more to his taste. The Stanze, begun by Raphael for Julius, were still to be completed, and when Bramante died in April 1514 he was succeeded as architect of St Peter's by Raphael. A new contract for the Tomb, drawn up on 6 May 1513, changed the whole design. Whether, at this juncture, the original project for a free-standing tomb in the new St Peter's had been abandoned cannot be decided, but since Michelangelo committed himself to finishing the work in seven years, and since the new St Peter's still only consisted of part of the crossing and a temporary structure protecting the papal altar at the end of the partially demolished nave, it is more than probable that the unlikelihood of the basilica being ready to receive the Tomb within the given time was already foreseen. To this must be added the practical realization that it might

81 MICHELANGELO Tomb of Julius II, S. Pietro in Vincoli

82 GIACOMO ROCCHETTI after MICHELANGELO Drawing of 1513 project for the tomb of Julius II

be difficult, years after Julius's death, to persuade whoever might then occupy the papal throne to consent to the erection of so large a monument in what would have to be a very prominent position.

The new contract abandoned the free-standing project in favour of a variant of the traditional wall-tomb, though on an unprecedented scale, and with only a slightly reduced amount of sculpture: Michelangelo described the project as larger than his original design, but the dimensions in the contract do not support this, except that a superstructure – the *cappelletta* – over the rectangular base now raised the height considerably over the original dimensions. Three drawings, besides the little sketches on the Libyan sheet, exist from this stage. One is a rough scrawl by Michelangelo (London, British Museum), made from memory in 1516; the others are two copies (Berlin, Kupferstichkabinett; Florence, Gabinetto Disegni e Stampe) differing in detail but showing basically the same arrangement of the lower part, the Berlin drawing alone showing the form of the proposed *cappelletta*. Neither drawing gives any indication that the monument was to be nearly twice as deep as it was wide, or that the total number of figures amounted to thirty-five, most of them being either life-sized, or, in the case of the *cappelletta* and the sepulchre with the effigy of the dead Julius, as much as twice life-size. To all this must be added the ornamental sculpture such as the herms, the arabesques on the spandrels and bases, the niche shells, and at least three reliefs either in bronze or in marble. *82*

Michelangelo had the marble prepared for the original project removed from his workshop adjacent to St Peter's to a house in the Macel de' Corvi which he retained from 1513 until his death (it was demolished when the ground was cleared for the Vittorio Emanuele monument), sent for three assistants from Florence – artisans rather than sculptors – and between May 1513 and July 1516 he carved the two *Slaves* and the *Moses*. All three figures stem from ideas developed in the Ceiling: the *Slaves* from the *Ignudi* and the *Moses* from the prophets. The two *Slaves* were part of a series of twelve, designed to represent the Arts as stricken, imprisoned, crushed, by the death of their patron and protector. The so-called *Dying Slave*, carried to a perfection of finish in every detail and heightened by the contrast with the rough curving form behind his legs which was intended to become a monkey ('painting as the aping of Nature'), epitomizes the artist's response to perfect male beauty and is a languid, sensual, relaxed, tender and hauntingly expressive hymn to the major passion of the sculptor's life. The *Rebellious Slave* is less highly finished, less poetic in conception, more thick-set physically compared with the expressive elegance of the *Dying Slave*. He struggles desperately against the bonds that imprison him and the fate which he realizes will overcome him, and his twisting movement, arrested by the bonds that chain him, emphasizes the development of the muscles of his arms and body. *83* *84*

Neither in pose nor in movement does either of the *Slaves* imitate the two sons of Laocoön, but the resemblances are there just the same in the exhausted yielding of one figure and the violent but forlorn struggle of the other. The third statue from this period is the majestic and awe-inspiring *Moses*. Originally, the rectangular lower block of the tomb, some 16 ft 6 in (5 m) wide and 28 ft 6 in (8·75 m) deep, was to have been surmounted by six statues, each twice life-size, but the *Moses* was the only one certainly carved by Michelangelo himself. The pose, with one leg advanced slightly in front of the other, the turn and immense prominence of the head, with its majestic flowing beard, the exaggeration of the facial expression, would not be so strikingly obvious were the figure seen at the height and distance which were envisaged and allowed for in its conception. Far more than any of the Ceiling *86*

83 MICHELANGELO *Dying Slave* 1513/16

84 MICHELANGELO *Rebellious Slave* 1513/16

85 Donatello *St John the Evangelist* 1410–15

86 (*right*) Michelangelo *Moses* 1513/16

prophets it is an embodiment of the character and role of the major Old Testament prophet, an expression of the *terribilità* of Moses, of the artist and of his indomitable patron. There have been many attempts at interpreting the meaning of the figure, ranging from Moses's rage at the Jews' idolatry of the Golden Calf to the symbolism of antique River Gods, to an anguished spiritual self-portrait, or the confrontation of the Active and Contemplative Life, for which a suitable companion figure is hypothesized. Whether these glosses are valid or even necessary is a matter of opinion. What is clear is the complete realization of the interpretation on the human and spiritual plane. *85* Memories of Donatello's *St John the Evangelist* are certainly present – no artist can escape his formative influences – but the development of Michelangelo's own pessimistic and tragic vision is now so overwhelming that all influences, whether of antique or modern works, are absorbed, submerged, subsumed.

87 MICHELANGELO *Risen Christ (Christ of the Minerva)* 1519/20

The other commission of the period was for the Roman church of Sta Maria sopra Minerva, for a figure of the *Risen Christ*. This the sculptor executed between 1514 and 1516, but when the statue was well advanced a flaw – a vein of dark marble – was revealed which disfigured Christ's face. Michelangelo abandoned the work, but later between 1519 and 1520 when in Florence he carved a replacement which was sent to Rome to be finished and erected in charge of an assistant, Pietro Urbano. Sebastiano del Piombo in September 1520 wrote to Michelangelo to have the work stopped because of Urbano's bungling, and the statue was then finished and placed in position by Federico Frizzi. It is Michelangelo's chief and perhaps only total failure, but one for which he cannot, perhaps, be blamed. In later years he wished, as an *ex voto*, to replace it, but the principal commissioner, Antonio Metello Vari, refused and asked instead for the original damaged statue, which he kept in his garden. Here it was recorded in 1556, but it then disappeared.

How much of the unsatisfactory quality of the figure is due to Urbano's over-zealous finishing is difficult to determine, but the rather awkward stance and the strained turn of the head must be Michelangelo's. It is a less exaggerated form of the *figura serpentinata* which is so strong a feature of the *Ignudi* of the Ceiling and of the *Rebellious Slave*, and which Michelangelo clearly used to endow his figures with vitality and movement. The figure of Christ, holding an emblematic cross and the reed and sponge of the last moments of the Passion, originally stood on a high pedestal against a shallow niche designed for it by Frizzi. This was altered in the early nineteenth century and the figure now stands against a pilaster, which enables it to be seen almost in the round, though this probably defeats the sculptor's intentions. The late sixteenth-century copy by Taddeo Landini in Sto Spirito in Florence gives a better idea of the original setting and effect of the statue.

By the time he died in 1513, Julius II had recovered almost all the territories alienated by Alexander VI, and had acquired Parma and Piacenza from the Sforza domains. But it had meant a virtually continuous state of war. Leo X decided on a different policy. He was thirty-seven years old at the time of his unexpected election, a placid, pleasure-loving man, prodigal and spendthrift, of blameless morals, with all the political astuteness of the Medici, physically of heavy build, with weak sight and suffering from incurable bowel trouble. His election was received with satisfaction everywhere in Europe, so that he started with the handicap that the rulers of Spain, France and the Empire all hoped to be able to sway him to their advantage. Six principles governed his policy:

The preservation of the integrity of the Papal States.
The restoration of Medici power in Florence and the establishment of a dynasty there, and hence the attachment of Florence to papal policies and the abandonment by Florence of her pro-French sympathies.
The prevention of the re-establishment of French power in northern Italy.
The prevention of the spread of Spanish power in the north of Italy.
The prevention of both Naples and the north of Italy coming under Spanish control, which would have left the Papal States caught between two areas of foreign domination.
The successful conclusion of the struggle with France over the schismatic Council of Pisa, and the submission of the cardinals involved in it.

Only in the second and the last of these aims was he successful.

The reign began badly with a new invasion by the French in 1513, but they were rapidly driven out of Italy again, and this defeat persuaded the French king to abandon his support of the schismatic cardinals, while bringing about their submission and the full recognition by the French of the validity of the Lateran Council. The attempt by Venice to recover Vicenza and Verona ended in her defeat by the Spanish Viceroy. Leo's alarm at the encroachment of foreign power was increased when the death of Louis XII of France was followed by the accession of Francis I. To avenge the defeats of his predecessor, Francis invaded Italy in 1515, captured Milan by October, and was so successful in his campaign that Leo agreed to meet him in Bologna in December to discuss a peace settlement.

In January 1516 Ferdinand of Aragon died and was succeeded by his grandson Charles V. The immediate danger from Spain was enormously increased by the fact that Charles V was also the grandson of the Emperor Maximilian, who was endeavouring to ensure that Charles should succeed him as Emperor. This meant that both Spain and Germany would be under the control of the same ruler, and moreover Naples was already a Spanish possession. Leo's internal difficulties were increased by the defection in 1516 of the Duke of Urbino, who openly sided with the French against the pope, so that Leo was forced into a war against the della Rovere – which he won quite quickly. He made his nephew Lorenzo de' Medici the new Duke of Urbino, but this brought him bitter reproaches from those who reminded him of the help and refuge so often given to the Medici by Urbino in times of trouble in Florence, and accusations that he had destroyed the della Rovere in order to increase Medici power in a policy of nepotism. Leo maintained, however, that to overlook so blatant a breach of faith by a major vassal would be interpreted as so great a sign of weakness that he would be faced with equally dangerous rebellions from other vassals, such as the pro-Spanish Colonna and the pro-French Orsini, and from Ferrara and Mantua, both states on his northern borders.

In order to prevent the election of Charles V of Spain as the successor of the Emperor Maximilian, who died in January 1519, Leo went to great lengths to obtain the crown for either the Elector of Saxony or the Elector of Brandenburg, and when this failed for Francis I of France, preferring to see the French king as Emperor, which he reckoned would keep him too busy to interfere in Italy, than to see the crown conferred on the Spanish king. He failed: Charles V was elected Emperor on 28 June 1519 and Leo's greatest fear was now an accomplished fact. These years also saw the first acts in the drama which was to engulf the Church and destroy the unity of Christendom.

The state of the Church in Germany had long been unsatisfactory. The recruitment of higher dignitaries exclusively from the nobility resulted in many major German sees becoming virtually hereditary prince-bishoprics, the see passing from uncle to nephew as an appanage of local family power, with the duties performed by surrogates. This bad example was copied down the line, so that the number of ecclesiastics was inflated and the revenues of the Church were diverted to secular ends. The replacement of old German law by Roman law from the fifteenth century onwards increased the bureaucracy and reduced the peasantry to total subjugation to their rulers, particularly when secular and religious powers were combined in the same office. One consequence was bitter opposition to Rome and a detestation of the Curia, the rapacity of whose tax-gatherers was seen as a major cause of local ills. Despite all the arguments that Rome was entitled to the financial support of the faithful throughout Christendom, the cry that Germany was bled white to support the luxury and worldliness of Rome was a potently emotive one, and in view of the frequent diversion to other less worthy objects of, for instance, tithes raised for a Crusade, and the stories brought back by pilgrims of the state of the Church in Rome, these grievances became a vivid theme which fired discontent and alienation. The matter was finally brought to a head by the preaching of indulgences.*

Julius II had proclaimed an indulgence for the building of St Peter's, but it had lapsed on his death. Despite warnings about the dangerous state of discontent over the raising of money in Germany, Leo renewed the indulgence for St Peter's soon after his accession. Unfortunately, the manner of its preaching and the division of the alms raised between the Church, the Emperor and Archbishop Albert of Brandenburg, so that Albert could pay off his debt to the banking house of Fugger, who had lent him large sums to pay the composition demanded by Leo for a dispensation to hold three major sees as a plurality, rapidly became a scandal. From this scandal arose the action of Luther, who on 31 October 1517 nailed his ninety-five theses attacking such abuses to the door of the castle church in Wittenberg, thus starting what eventually became a total breach between Rome and a large part of northern Europe.

The preaching of the indulgence was stopped late in 1518, but the damage was done. Leo at first failed to recognize the acute danger that Luther represented, his mind being filled with anxieties over the Imperial election, and though moves were made against Luther the popular support for his anti-Rome, anti-papal attitudes was such that he soon advocated the total rejection of the Church. He was excommunicated in January 1521, but it was almost impossible to publish this in Germany because opposition to Luther

* When a penitent sinner confesses and receives absolution, the act of absolution removes the guilt of the sin, but not, of course, any temporal punishment which may have been incurred. The Church has always claimed the right to alleviate the pains of Purgatory if the penitent performs good works as an earnest of intentions. Such works could, for example, be the contribution of money to the rebuilding of St Peter's. It is easy to see how Luther could then claim that indulgences were for sale.

was held to be part of a Roman and Italian campaign, whereas Luther was a German patriot protesting about German grievances against the Curia, Rome and the pope.

Projects for some grand work to mark the restoration of Medici power in Florence in 1512 must have been in the minds of Leo X and the family representative in Florence, Leo's nephew Lorenzo de' Medici, from the time of Leo's election in 1513, despite the unpropitious political situation. On 1 December 1515 Leo made a triumphal entry into Florence on his way to Bologna to meet Francis I of France. He returned to Florence on 22 December and remained there until at least the end of January. The project for a façade to cover the unfinished rough stone front of S. Lorenzo, the Medici parish church built by Brunelleschi, was probably first conceived in 1515. Vasari lists the participants in a competition, or rather in an enterprise of collaboration between several artists, which he states was to be under Michelangelo's direction, as Raphael, Andrea and Jacopo Sansovino, Baccio d'Agnolo, and Antonio da Sangallo the Elder. This list is inaccurate. It was Antonio da Sangallo's brother Giuliano, who had retired because of ill-health from the works at the new St Peter's and had returned to Florence in 1515, who prepared drawings for the project. Vasari's statement that Raphael was sent for to discuss the project while the pope was in Florence is certainly wrong; Andrea Sansovino cannot positively be connected with the project; Baccio d'Agnolo is stated, in Vasari's Life of Jacopo Sansovino, to have been only the executant of Sansovino's model. If Leo saw designs for the façade during his stay in Florence they must have been those by Jacopo Sansovino, who was working in Florence at the time, and by Giuliano da Sangallo. Of the Sangallo drawings, two are signed, one has the Medici arms and a statue of Leo on the top, and two are dated 1516, which means that they were done after Leo's visit, since the Florentine year started on 25 March. Giuliano was eliminated from the affair by his death in October 1516.

88

Despite both Condivi's and Vasari's assertions that Michelangelo was involved in the project from the start, there is little evidence to support this; in fact, Leo must have envisaged a joint enterprise and have promised Sansovino – no mean sculptor – a part of the commission, since in June 1517 Sansovino in an angry letter to Michelangelo accused him of dishonesty, malice and jealousy. Clearly, once the commission was available Michelangelo determined to have it, without assistants or collaborators, all of which suggests that his part in the transaction was by no means as blameless, nor were his protestations of unwillingness as sincere, as his biographers make out.

By 1516 the position of the della Rovere family had changed dramatically, since in March 1516 the duke had been deprived of his duchy. Were Michelangelo to be relieved of the incubus of the Tomb, he would then be free to undertake the major commission now obtainable in his native Florence. On 8 July 1516 a new contract was signed for the Tomb which again whittled it down in size and reduced the number of figures still to be carved. Michelangelo was in Carrara in July 1516 extracting marble for the Tomb; but by November the commission for the façade was apparently his, since some of the marble was for the façade, which he was to execute in conjunction with Baccio d'Agnolo, whose first model made by 7 March 1517 was rejected by Michelangelo as 'childish'. By May 1517 Baccio d'Agnolo had been dropped from the commission and the second model, made by Michelangelo in clay, was a misshapen affair. On the basis of this model, however, the estimate of the cost rose from 25,000 to 35,000 ducats. Between 31 August 1517 and December 1517 Michelangelo in Florence executed another model with twenty-four figures in wax, and on 19 January 1518 in Rome he signed the contract for the façade based on the last model. Already in 1517 he had been ordered to extract his marble from new quarries at Pietrasanta, in Florentine territory, rather than obtaining it from Carrara, and his protests about the inaccessibility of these new quarries, the unsatisfactory quality of the marble, and the difficulties of obtaining workmen and transport were brushed aside with the accusation that they were prompted by private agreement with the Marquis of Carrara, which was true in that the marquis and Michelangelo were on terms of friendship. Firstly, he had to make a road from the quarries to Seravezza, and then when he had extracted marble the barges he hired at Pisa never arrived – probably the first well-organized retaliatory boycott to protect the virtual monopoly held by Carrara for the exploitation of its major asset. From being a friend, the marquis turned against Michelangelo and refused to allow him even to have the marble which had already been cut from his quarries. Also, he had endless trouble both with the protesting della Rovere, and with the building of a house with a suitable workshop. Then suddenly early in 1520 the whole project lapsed, and the contract was abruptly cancelled. Michelangelo was furious, and in March 1520 he wrote angrily to a friend in bitter complaint over his lost time, the money he had spent in establishing himself in Florence, and the insult he felt he had suffered.

What would Michelangelo's façade have looked like? In many ways it was like most of his other works: an extension, a recasting of his thinking, in this case of the Julius Tomb. The problem of designing a unified classical façade for a church where the nave formed a high central projection with lean-to roofs for chapels or aisles had first been faced by Alberti in 1450 at

88 Giuliano da Sangallo Drawing for the façade of S. Lorenzo

S. Francesco in Rimini when he converted the Gothic church into the Renaissance Tempio Malatestiana. Alberti based the lower part of his façade on a triumphal arch, an idea which he repeated on a grander scale in his design for the façade of S. Andrea in Mantua in 1472, where the triumphal arch involves the whole façade and encloses a narthex. It is unlikely that Michelangelo knew either of these churches except by hearsay, although they were seminal in design. He must, however, have known Giuliano da Sangallo's designs for the S. Lorenzo façade (Giuliano was a close friend), and all these included a lower storey based on a triumphal arch system with three portals separated by orders of columns; two of them had nartheces in the lower storey and high temple fronts covering the projecting nave gable, two others with high projections had a mezzanine area between the base and the superimposed temple front of the nave gable, and another two not only used the same triumphal arch form below, but extended it above into a unified façade like a palace front, concealing the aisles behind a free-standing upper storey. Giuliano's projects were influenced by his familiarity with designs prepared for the new St Peter's, since one of his drawings has the façade flanked by two tall towers, of the 'Tower of the Orders' type (i.e. a different Order of columns from Doric to Composite from base to top),

88

89 MICHELANGELO Sketch for the façade of S. Lorenzo 1517

90 MICHELANGELO Wooden model for the façade of S. Lorenzo 1517

much as was used by his brother Antonio at S. Biagio in Montepulciano, the idea stemming from Bramante's design for St Peter's as it is known from the 1506 medal.

89 There are three early designs by Michelangelo, all with a high central feature projecting above a two-storey base, the lower part of which has the triumphal arch form. One of these can be dated by a draft for a letter which he wrote between 13 and 16 January 1517, which means that they were designed before he developed the narthex scheme, worked out in the clay model in the first week of May 1517 and which occasioned the steep rise in the estimate. The idea of the narthex, made by giving the façade one return bay at the sides, possibly stemmed from one of Giuliano's drawings, but was certainly prompted by the unsatisfactory look a free-standing façade rising above the aisles would have presented from the sides and rear. This sort of screen façade existed at Orvieto Cathedral and also at S. Michele in Lucca, both of which Michelangelo almost certainly knew. The model in the Casa *90* Buonarroti, Florence, has had a chequered career, in that only recently has it been decided that it is not a much later recension of Michelangelo's various designs, but is the model made probably by Urbano in 1517 and therefore represents Michelangelo's final decision (in so far as any design of his was ever final). It incorporates the unified palace front, the triumphal arch motive, and the narthex, with a slight emphasis on the central bay. The model looks cold and dry, but even though it was never executed it is important as Michelangelo's first fully worked-out major architectural scheme and it had a vital place both in his own architecture and in its influence on his contemporaries and successors. His earlier essays in architecture had been limited to the much-altered fragment of the façade of the chapel in Castel S. Angelo, and the so-called 'kneeling windows' inserted into the arches of the street-level loggia of the Medici palace. These heavy windows, borne on large consoles, were done about 1517, and established a fashion which survived into this century.

Lorenzo de' Medici, Duke of Urbino from 1516, died in Florence in May 1519, aged only twenty-eight, a few weeks after his young wife had died in childbirth leaving a daughter, Catherine, who later became Queen of France. His uncle, Giuliano, Duke of Nemours through his marriage with a princess of Savoy, had died in 1516 at the age of thirty-eight, and with them was extinguished the direct line of the Medici from Cosimo Pater Patriae. From now on the family proceeded from the collateral branch stemming from Lorenzo, Cosimo's younger brother. The death of Lorenzo of Urbino, which ended the dynastic hopes of Leo X, was clearly the mainspring of the project to build a family funerary chapel in S. Lorenzo, and probably also prompted the cancellation of the façade project, although it appears that the chapel was being planned and the site cleared before the abandonment of the façade project. The earliest record is by Giovanni Battista Figiovanni, then a Canon of S. Lorenzo and Prior from 1534 onwards, who says in his memoirs that in June 1519 Cardinal Giulio de' Medici, who had come to Florence to the deathbed of Lorenzo of Urbino, told him '. . . we are of a mind to spend about 50,000 ducats on S. Lorenzo, the library and the sacristy to match the one already made, which will be called a chapel, where there will be many tombs in which to bury our dead forefathers: Lorenzo, Giuliano our father, and Giuliano and Lorenzo, brother and nephew.' He added that he hoped Figiovanni would be the administrator of the project.

The question of how far Michelangelo was responsible for the exterior structure of the New Sacristy (or Medici Chapel) has long been controversial. Condivi does not mention the construction of the chapel itself; Vasari merely says that 'he vaulted the cupola which may be seen there', and then continues about the interior and the making of four tombs. But from an appraisal of the few facts, and from a very careful examination of the building itself, the following conclusions may be reached.

93

101

The site was determined by the space on the right side of the church – the north side, since S. Lorenzo has a reversed orientation – in the angle between the transept and the choir corresponding to Brunelleschi's Old Sacristy, begun exactly a hundred years earlier on the opposite side of the choir. The site had been built over, and two houses were demolished in November 1519 to clear part of it, but other houses on the site remained and were allowed for in the building of the chapel. On 1 March 1520 the chapter made a grant towards the building costs, and work on the foundations began. At about the same time a stonemason submitted an estimate for the construction of the *pietra serena* interior pilasters and cornices on the model of the Old Sacristy. Michelangelo's first project for the chapel was laid before Cardinal Giulio on 23 November, but a further plan exists for the central space with one carefully drawn apsidal chapel, which was almost certainly a first idea for the altar space, and with two other roughly scrawled similar shapes on two other sides of the chapel. This would never have been practicable given the other buildings on the site, but that Michelangelo should have even considered such an idea indicates that he was almost certainly in control of the structure after the foundation stage. By April 1521 part of the *pietra serena* work had been started and Michelangelo's first design for the tombs had been approved. There had been some discussion about the traditional type of wall-tomb, but the first project was for a free-standing monument in the centre of the chapel. This presented the difficulty that it would have had to be very small to avoid overcrowding the chapel. Later, the cardinal himself proposed a monument on the model of the Roman antique gateway of the

91 (*left*) Section and plan of the Old Sacristy, S. Lorenzo

92 (*right*) Section and plan of the New Sacristy (Medici Chapel), S. Lorenzo

arcus quadrifons, with four sarcophagi over four arches, and with a fifth space in the centre, destined for the cardinal himself. But this design was impractical and all these schemes were discarded in favour of a double tomb facing the altar, and single tombs on the side walls. The marble for all three monuments was ordered in the second half of April 1521 – from Carrara incidentally. It must have been well before this date that Michelangelo worked out his ideas for the upper part of the chapel, inserting the extra attic storey between the central cubic space and the pendentives below the dome. There is no reason for the existence of this extra storey, which departs radically from the model of the Old Sacristy, unless extra height were required by the design of the tombs and by the projects for the painted

100 *92* *91*

93 S. Lorenzo, view of façade with Medici Chapel (right)

decoration of the chapel (which was never executed). This mezzanine area, or attic storey, clearly reflects the Pantheon, where such a storey exists (indeed the Medici Chapel is another Pantheon – a resting place for the illustrious dead), and follows the Roman original in the form of the dome, which is coffered like the Pantheon with an *oculus* at the top, though here it is covered by the high lantern on the outside of the dome. Michelangelo took particular trouble with the design of the lantern, which is like a tiny colonnaded temple recalling that of Brunelleschi's Old Sacristy, but made deliberately more complex.

The wall between the church and the chapel was also rebuilt, and a wall which formed one side of a passage leading to an entrance door in the transept was removed, since it encumbered the space in which the chapel was to be built (Figiovanni says that the demolitions were of '. . . two houses of the Nelli family and the walls of the church in that part where the chapel was to be built').* This enabled Michelangelo to plan the door into the church at an angle to accord with the internal arrangement of his architecture, and also allowed him to hollow out a deep niche to contain the double tomb projected for Lorenzo the Magnificent and his brother Giuliano, as well as the *Madonna and Child* and the two patron saints.

* I am indebted to Miss Caroline Elam for a sight of the early plan (made before the Medici Chapel was started), discovered by Mr Howard Burns in the archives in Venice. This plan justified my statement that the wall between the church and the chapel was rebuilt, and added the information about the passageway to the transept door. A full discussion of the building of the chapel is to be published by Miss Elam in the *Mitteilungen des Kunsthistorischen Institutes in Florenz*, together with an appraisal of the newly discovered plan of S. Lorenzo by Mr Burns.

The plan of the chapel has another important feature in that the interior has eight doors, two in each angle of the walls. Two doors open to the vestries or *lavamani* flanking the altar, one gives into the church (this was originally the only entrance; the present arrangement of the door on the other side is a modern one to enable visitors to reach the chapel without passing through the church), and the other five were blind, inserted for symmetry and not for any function. When all the doors are shut, the chapel is an entirely enclosed space; the altar faces inwards into the chapel, instead of being at the back of the little choir against the wall, as in Brunelleschi's Old Sacristy. The tombs are surmounted by the figures of the dead, who look towards the *Madonna and Child* on the end wall; the priest saying the Mass or the Office for the Dead would be doing so in an enclosed space in which his congregation is the dead, who look towards the group of the *Madonna and Child* which forms the altarpiece, symbolically over the altar, but in fact on the far side of the chapel. On either side of the *Madonna and Child* the two Medici patron saints, *Cosmas* and *Damian*, present their votaries and intercede for them.

94

95, 96

99

The interior architecture of the chapel is complicated, for between his first designs for the S. Lorenzo façade and those for the Medici Chapel Michelangelo's attitude towards architectural form, and his interest in and feeling for it, underwent a very great development. In one of his most powerful passages, Vasari expatiates on the variety and novelty of the architectural forms invented for, and introduced into, the Medici Chapel, commenting on Michelangelo's departure from accepted classical forms, his unwillingness to be bound by the models of the ancients, and his insistence on the equal validity of his own powers of invention against the rules and patterns handed down from antiquity. Vasari also remarks on the effect this had on other men, who imitated his licence and freedom without possessing his sense of fitness and control: '. . . new kinds of fantastic ornamentation containing more of the grotesque than of rule or reason' is how he puts it, reflecting wryly on the consequences of Michelangelo's departures from 'common usage and . . . Vitruvius and the works of Antiquity'. For instance, one of the strange features of the area above the extra attic storey is the unusual form of the windows, which are heavily pedimented and narrower at the top than at the bottom, so that they increase the perspective effect of the extra height given by the additional storey. Within the strong framework of the *pietra serena* pilasters and architraves which stress the structural features of the chapel, the levels of the marble revetment round the two tombs form a complex arrangement of layers, with deep and shallow niches adjacent, pediments jammed tightly into framing members, and recessions and projections which create diversity in depth and surface. Over

94 MICHELANGELO Medici Chapel, 1520–34, view looking towards entrance wall

95 MICHELANGELO Tomb of Giuliano de' Medici

96 MICHELANGELO Tomb of Lorenzo de' Medici

94 the eight doors are tabernacles of greater size and complexity than the 95, 96 doorways themselves; the statues of the two dukes are within niches only barely large enough to contain them, flanked by shallow recesses originally intended to hold other allegorical figures which would have projected beyond their niches. The sarcophagi seem crushed by the size of the figures reclining upon them, and in the original designs there were to have been four figures of River Gods, below the sarcophagi, so as to create a pyramidal design on either wall.

The symbolism of the chapel is complex, a mixture of Christian and classical: at ground-level the River Gods would have represented the zone of the Underworld; the four Times of Day – Dawn and Dusk, Night and Day – represent the zone of the transient World; the figures of the dead, translated into another sphere and idealized beyond their earthly condition, represent the Heavenly domain to which the dead have attained.

The dead are indeed idealized. They are depicted in Roman armour, 95, 96 Giuliano bare-headed, alert and tense, as the Active Life; Lorenzo, his helmet shadowing his face, relaxed, with the reflective gesture of his hand covering his mouth, as the Contemplative Life. Below Giuliano are the positive Times of Day – Night and Day – and below Lorenzo are the indecisive Times of

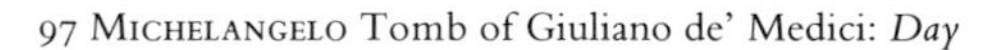

97 MICHELANGELO Tomb of Giuliano de' Medici: *Day*

98 MICHELANGELO Tomb of Giuliano de' Medici: *Night*

Day – Dawn and Dusk – the earthly counterparts of the states of mind they represent. Formerly the actual lighting of the chapel stressed these states, in that the windows over Lorenzo were shadowed, so that his side of the chapel received only filtered light, while the windows over Giuliano shed their light fully on the interior, but later this arrangement was changed to give the present even light. The ornamental detail of the architecture also carries on the funerary symbolism, consisting of rams' skulls, small masks, garlands of laurels, vases, candelabra – all graveyard symbols, all varied with infinite versatility and richness of invention. The massive figures on the sarcophagi are also richly symbolic: *Night*, with her deeply shadowed head and diadem crowned with a horned moon and a star, the hollow-eyed mask below her shoulder, the owl crouching beneath her leg; *Day*, only just emerging from the block, so that half his face is still submerged in the marble, gazing with head erect and with body tensed for movement; *Dawn*, struggling as if in a tragic renewal of consciousness, dragged reluctantly and with an expression of intense grief on her face into the awareness of another day; *Dusk*, sinking relaxed into passivity and torpor, as if age as well as grief

98

97

99 MICHELANGELO *Madonna and Child*

100 (*right*) MICHELANGELO Sketch for a double tomb 1520/21

had finally defeated him. None of the figures is finished; all emerge from the block in partial completion, yet they are fully realized as ideas, and as forms. The two dukes are completely finished (even the backs of the figures were worked as fully as the fronts), and while Lorenzo's gesture recalls the pensive *Jeremiah* of the Sistine Ceiling, Giuliano takes up the pose of the vigorous *Moses* with only slight changes in the position of the arms and hands.

54

86

94, 99

On the 'altar wall' opposite the altar, the *Madonna and Child* and the patron saints form the altarpiece – a typical *Sacra Conversazione*. Adapted perhaps from a classical figure of a Muse, the grave and introspective Madonna sits cross-legged with the energetic Child straddling her knee to turn and bury His face in her breast. The block is exceptionally deep and unusually narrow for so complex a movement. The group is Michelangelo's final statement in sculpture of the theme of the Madonna and Child. The Madonna's face is almost as tragic as the reluctant Dawn, full of foreboding as she gazes into the space before her, hearing with resigned acceptance the

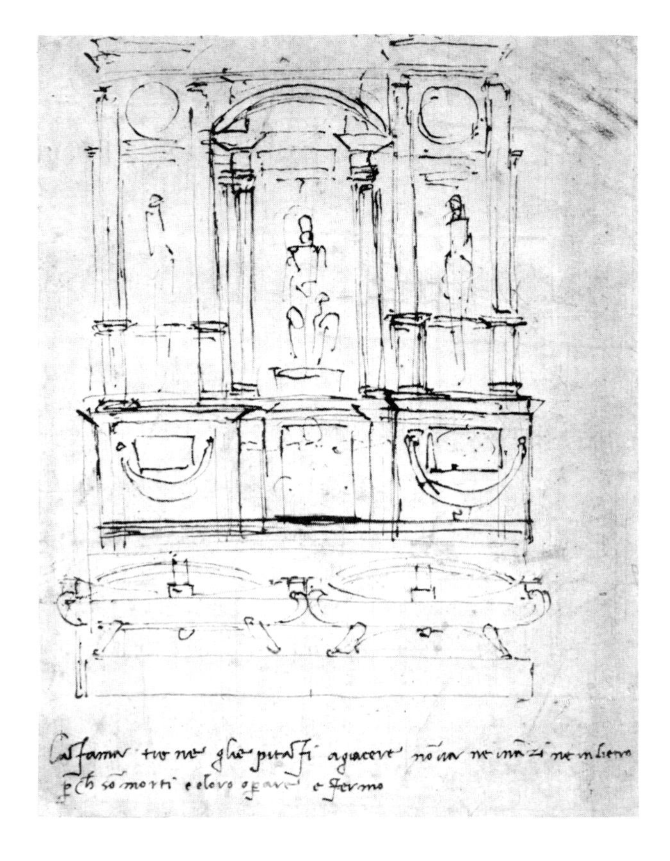

recurrent Office of the Dead and the commemoration of the Sacrifice of the vigorous Child she holds, who Himself seems to turn away from the prospect of His own mission. The two saints are the work of assistants, though Michelangelo may have indicated their design and sketched the Laocoön type of the head of Cosmas. Not only are they feeble, but they are now in the wrong positions, since they ought rightly to be turned towards the dukes whom they should invite to approach the Madonna and Child, instead of turning away from the men whom they protect.

There is evidence that a fresco decoration was also planned for the chapel, and that the lunettes over the tombs were to have continued the celestial zone into the theme of the Resurrection, but this part of the project came to nothing. The dating of the two tombs is fairly clear: the architecture was not complete until 1524, when the dome was finished. Later, a stucco decoration by Giovanni da Udine, for which Michelangelo made a drawing, was applied to it, but ultimately Vasari whitewashed it over. By June 1524 the

101 MICHELANGELO Medici Chapel, view of cupola

tomb of Lorenzo was well advanced, and it was completed by June 1526. The tomb of Giuliano was probably made between 1531 and 1533; while the remaining tomb, that of Lorenzo the Magnificent and his brother, was apparently begun in August 1533. This last was abandoned when Michelangelo left Florence for Rome in 1534, but before he left the statues of the two dukes had both been placed in their niches. The Bull establishing the memorial services was issued by Clement VII in November 1532; it provided for three daily Masses, and a continuous recital of the Psalter and special prayers for the dead, to be recited by four newly appointed chaplains and the canons of S. Lorenzo. The services, however, cannot have started at once, since none of the figures on the sarcophagi had been erected at this time, but were lying in various stages of completion on the floor of the chapel. They were finally assembled by Tribolo and Montelupo in 1545, and a certain amount of finishing – though mercifully little – was done. The project was a victim of the political events of the time, for by 1534 Michelangelo's deep patriotism had turned from pride in the greatness of the Medici to a profound revulsion against the family he had once admired and served. The full extent of his feeling is found in the famous quatrain he sent in reply to an admirer who had praised the *Night* as so lifelike that if one spoke to her she would awaken:

> *Sweet to me is sleep, and even more to be of stone*
> *While wrong and shame endure;*
> *Not to see, nor to hear is my good fortune.*
> *Therefore, do not wake me; speak softly here.*

The idea of a library to hold the manuscripts collected by Lorenzo the Magnificent, which had hitherto been kept in the Medici palace, dates back to 1519, the same time as the decision about the funerary chapel, but nothing was done about it until immediately after Cardinal Giulio's election as Clement VII. Michelangelo recorded in a letter of 2 January 1524 that the pope desired to have a design for libraries to contain the manuscripts, but that he still did not know where they were to be built. At first, there were discussions about two sites. One was within the convent of S. Lorenzo with direct access from the piazza, which would have been convenient for building and for later use, but this was rejected because it impinged too much upon the convent itself. The second site was at right angles to the church, parallel with the north side of the convent and projecting deeply into the piazza, but it was finally abandoned in favour of building the new library on the model of the one at the convent of S. Marco in Florence – that is, over existing buildings so as to protect it against damp and to ensure a good light. The refectory range of the monastery was selected, and the refectory itself was vaulted in fireproof materials. The structural system was novel, in that *102* strong buttresses were constructed which would enable the actual walls to be made into thin screens between the piers, thus concentrating the strength of the building in a series of cells, which served also as the bays to which the reading-desks of the carrels were attached, with windows in the walls between the buttresses. In order to reach the library a staircase leads up to the upper storey of the cloister where a door gives into a high vestibule – the *103* *ricetto* – from which a free-standing staircase rises to the entrance doorway of *104* the library proper. The advantage of this system is that once the foundations

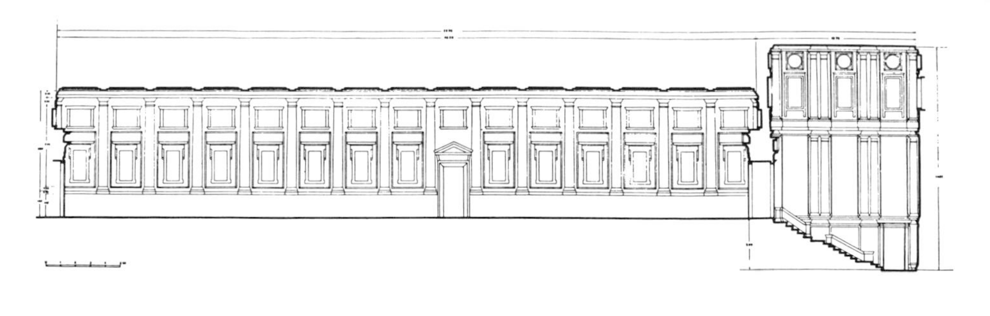

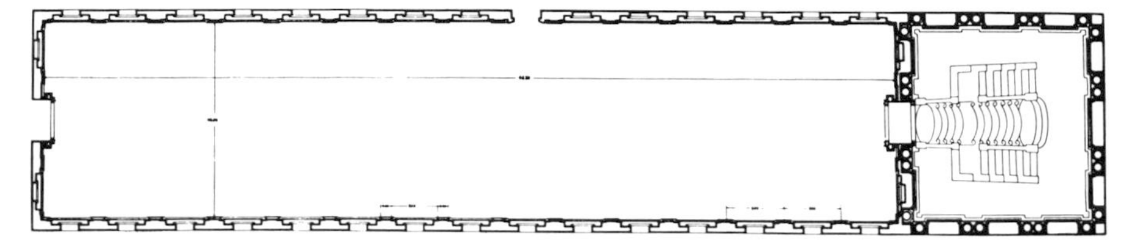

102 MICHELANGELO Laurenziana Library, begun 1524, section and plan

103 (*below*) MICHELANGELO Laurenziana Library, vestibule wall

104 (*right*) MICHELANGELO Laurenziana Library, vestibule staircase

had been laid and the vaulting of the refectory finished, the monastic quarters could return to use while the rest of the building work continued above. The structural system was approved by May 1524, the foundations were begun in July, and during the winter work continued on the substructure. In April 1525 the long walls of the library and the exterior window-frames were built. It was proposed to build a small 'chapel' at one end as a rare book room, and the vestibule staircase was planned as a single flight. The decision to raise the height of the vestibule by about another 4 ft (1.2 m) was taken in December, in order to light the area better. Michelangelo wanted to light the *ricetto* with skylights, but the pope rejected this idea, saying that he had no intention of having friars perpetually cleaning windows. Eventually the walls were raised more than the proposed two *braccia*, but the work was abandoned before the windows were installed, and the present ones date from the nineteenth century, when the articulation of the upper part of the *ricetto* was completed, and the modern rare book annex was built.

The staircase was not built according to Michelangelo's designs either. *104* When he left Florence in 1534 there was apparently no permanent stair from the vestibule into the library, and neither was the reading-room ceiling finished. The ceiling was not completed until 1549–50, when the floor was

also redesigned, and the staircase was commissioned from Ammanati by Duke Cosimo I in 1558–59. Michelangelo sent a model and instructions from Rome to Vasari, who was supervising the work, but the present free-standing staircase, which flows like lava from the library door into the vestibule, is perhaps more Ammanati than Michelangelo.

106 The reading-room is reasonably traditional in type: a long narrow room with three seats to each bay on either side, each with its sloping reading-desk designed by Michelangelo. The ceiling design is in large coffered bays corresponding to the buttresses, which are emphasized by the *pietra serena* pilasters resting on a string-course above the tops of the desks and supporting a narrow architrave below the ceiling. There are two windows to each bay, both with fine *pietra serena* frames, the lower one set within a panel which shows how thin the actual wall is. The door at the end, giving on to the vestibule, is a typically Michelangelesque device of a doorcase with a triangular pediment crowded into an outer framework with a segmental pediment, which is itself crowded within the space between the two framing pilasters. The effect is one of complexity and richness achieved with the most *103, 104* economical means. The vestibule is full of surprises. The beautiful contrast between white plaster and the brownish *pietra serena* – that favourite Florentine building stone – is used to create an extraordinary result. The accusations so often levelled at Michelangelo – that the architecture of the library is wayward, that the columns embedded in the wall suggest the antithesis of their proper function and are an unparalleled example of the artist's willingness to break the rules for mere effect (Burckhardt went so far

105 Giovanni Battista Piranesi Tomb of Annia Regilla, etching (detail) from the *Magnificenza . . . de' Romani*, 1761

106 MICHELANGELO Laurenziana Library, reading-room

as to call the vestibule 'an incomprehensible joke') – are completely wide of the mark in that these condemnations ignore the structural solution to the whole building. In the reading-room the pilasters mark the buttresses or piers which support the building; in the *ricetto* the piers are slightly recessed and the wall panels are allowed to project in front of them. But in the part above the lower string-course the piers are replaced by the paired columns which, though they are recessed behind the wall panels, are the main structural members carrying the upper part of the vestibule; in fact the columns replace the piers so that they are the piers made visible and turned to decorative account. As if to stress this functional quality the architrave over the capitals of the columns is also recessed, and then allowed to project over the wall panels between the pairs of columns. Each of the three wall panels has a blind tabernacle window of *pietra serena* with alternating pediments – triangular in the centre panel and segmental on either side – and the narrow pilaster frames of these windows introduce yet another feature which Michelangelo invented here and which he continued to develop in his later architectural designing: the pilasters, called *stipiti*, are narrower at the bottom than at the top (an inversion of normal form) and instead of having recognizable capitals they are crowned at the top by small brackets supporting the framework of the pediments, while at the bottom they project as small brackets or consoles to support visually the base of the window. The window-frames themselves form recesses with further mouldings inside and with a projecting plinth at the bottom, giving the impression that they were designed to have a vase or statue in them, though there is no evidence of any such intention. Above the windows are rectangular recesses with decorative mouldings and a flat hood moulding with narrow swags over it, and below the pairs of columns are large consoles which give the visual impression of supporting the columns, though in fact they are purely decorative features.

Despite its apparent novelty the idea of columns embedded in a wall has an antique origin. The second-century tomb of Annia Regilla on the Via Appia Antica outside Rome has, on one wall, a pair of columns, one round, one octagonal, separated and flanked by wall panels, so that the columns supporting the architrave are inserted or embedded in the wall which is hollowed out round them. The wall panels accompanying the columns have rectangular windows in them and these windows once had elaborate decorative terracotta frames to them, forms which must have had strong repercussions later on when Michelangelo came to design the attic storey windows of St Peter's. These window-framings have now gone, but can be seen in one of Piranesi's etchings in the *Magnificenza . . . de' Romani* of 1761. Equally important is a drawing in Giuliano da Sangallo's sketchbook of antique monuments and architectural details, which shows another tomb on the Via Appia, where two columns are both set within the encircling wall flanking a projecting wall panel containing a shell niche (Barberini Codex, 70 v). There is little doubt that Michelangelo knew Giuliano's sketchbook.

105

During the time that he was working in Florence the della Rovere family continued to press him for the completion of the Julius Tomb. For this he began a series of *Slaves*, or *Prisoners*, none of them finished or even more than partially freed from their enveloping blocks. He began five of these *Prisoners*, four now in the Accademia in Florence, one in the Casa Buonarroti, Florence, each one, in its present state, larger than the two *Slaves* already completed: none was eventually used for the Tomb. All are figures in contorted poses, muscular, thick-limbed, with none of the elegance of the *Dying Slave*, nor the pathos of the *Rebellious Slave*. They present fascinating evidence of his working methods; it is known that he worked normally from

107

83, 84

107 MICHELANGELO *Bearded Slave*

the front of the block, freeing the figure which he always considered to be imprisoned within the marble. These *Slaves* or *Prisoners* exemplify this method of working perhaps more fully than any other figures of his, since it is possible to distinguish which were intended to be seen straight on, and which were intended to be corner figures, presenting two viewpoints, like the *Rebellious Slave* in the earlier pair. Among other figures carved during the work on the Medici Chapel is the *Victory*, which formed part of the original project according to Vasari, and may in fact have been begun during work on the first project, though the highly developed *contrapposto* suggests a date in the 1520s rather than one in the first decade of the century. In its

108

108 MICHELANGELO *Victory c.* 1530/33

elegance the figure recalls the *Dying Slave* or the *Ignudi* of the Ceiling, and the heavy vanquished victim beneath his knee follows the bearded type of the *Prisoners* with which it is probably contemporary. The arguments over its meaning have thrown up endless interpretations, from political allusions to the reconquests by Julius II of the lost Papal States (untenable in the 1520s however apposite it might have been in 1505 or 1513), to the victory of youth over age, to the more traditional ideas of the victory of Virtue over Vice, with which interpretation the rough clay model of two struggling figures (Florence, Casa Buonarroti) has been associated. This clay group was probably begun in connection with a proposal by Soderini for a pendant to the *David*, but was later abandoned. It has been variously described as *Samson and the Philistine*, or *Hercules and Cacus*, but it is possible that it was also conceived as a pendant to the *Victory* destined for the Tomb. The *Victory*, despite the turning pose of the figure, is still designed to be seen from the front – from a single viewpoint, or at most from a very restricted angle of vision – and the development of the movement is contrived within these

109 MICHELANGELO *Apollo (David)* c. 1530

very narrow limits with the most consummate brilliance. Like the *David* of twenty years earlier, the effect is achieved by contrasting the turn of the body and the movement of the arm, with the turn of the head and the direction of the gaze, thus creating the impression of a multiple viewpoint which the block itself does not support. Another figure from this period is the *Apollo*, sometimes also called *David*, which Michelangelo, probably during the period 1528–30, began for Baccio Valori, an unsavoury political nominee of the Medici whom the sculptor, after the disasters of the siege of Florence, may have felt it prudent to conciliate. But when the man was appointed governor of the Romagna work on the figure lapsed, and it ended, like most of the work abandoned in Florence in 1534, in the Medici collections. Even the identification of the subject remains unexplained. Stylistically, the work fits in with the later period of the Medici Chapel both in the physical type and because it continues the exploration by the sculptor of the theme of the figure in suppressed movement with one arm raised to isolate the head from the direction of the body, a theme which begins in his painting with the *Doni*

109

Tondo, continues with the *Delphic Sibyl* and with *Jonah*, and with several of the *Ignudi* in the Ceiling, and first appears in sculpture in the *Christ of the Minerva*.

Leo's policy had been dictated by his fear on the one hand of domination by Imperial power, and on the other of finding himself controlled by France. Consistently, he played one side against the other in a policy of skilful double-dealing, and he resisted as best he could encroachments on the Papal States by Venice, and by acquisitive vassals, such as Ferrara. His chief minister was his cousin, Cardinal Giulio de' Medici, and when Leo died unexpectedly at the age of forty-six on 1 December 1521, Cardinal Giulio was the favourite candidate for the succession to the Holy See. Leo was hardly dead when Ferrara retook the disputed territories, Francesco Maria della Rovere retook Urbino, and the Baglioni retook Perugia. After fourteen days the Conclave reached deadlock, and on 9 January 1522 Cardinal Giulio suggested that the cardinals should look outside the ranks of those gathered in Rome, and proposed the Netherlander, Adrian Florenz., who was then Viceroy in Spain, and had at one time been tutor to Charles V. To everyone's astonishment, and to the vociferous dismay of the Romans outside the doors, he was elected, but because of great difficulties in travel he did not reach Rome until 29 August 1522, and when he finally arrived it was to find Rome in the grip of plague.

He broke with tradition by retaining his own name as Adrian VI, and he brought to his new dignity his simplicity of life, his austere frugality, and strong intentions for the reform of the Church. In Italian popular opinion he figured throughout his reign as a detested and uncultured barbarian, unable to understand, much less adapt to, the expectations held about the public role of the papacy. His reign was marked by a total end to artistic patronage (always so strong a feature of Leo's court), except for work on St Peter's which continued in a desultory manner after the death of Raphael in 1520. It was also characterized by a minute court largely composed of Netherlanders, drastic cuts in the papal civil service and offices, fruitless efforts to end the war between the Emperor and the French and their allies, unsuccessful attempts to counter the growing strength of the Lutheran heresy, and the futile promotion of a crusade against the Turks. Despite his former position in the Imperial household, Adrian remained as neutral as his difficult position allowed, and he endeavoured to favour neither the Imperialists nor the French, which naturally antagonized both. The quarrels between the Florentines, Cardinal Soderini and Cardinal Giulio, were so violent that the Medici cardinal retired to Florence from October 1522 until Soderini's pro-French and basically anti-papal policy foundered and Cardinal Giulio was recalled in April 1523. Adrian died on 14 September 1523, his death being hailed by the Romans as a deliverance.

After a bitter Conclave lasting fifty days, Cardinal Giulio finally emerged as Pope Clement VII on 19 November. His election was greeted with joy, particularly by artists and literary men, who hoped that a new age of Leo had dawned. He was a hardworking man, of strict morals, cold, serious, frugal, and faced with an empty treasury. Because of his position as Leo's right-hand man in the execution of his adroitly directed policies of neutrality, it came as a shock to his entourage to discover that as pope Clement was indecisive and irresolute, suspicious and procrastinating, with the awful defect of being swayed by whoever was the last to have his ear. In December 1524 he reluctantly sided with the French, who had had a run of military successes, and had to admit this to Charles V in January 1525, excusing himself because the French had also entered Naples by sea. Charles was furious at what he considered to be a betrayal, and even threatened Clement with Luther. But the French alliance was a disaster, since a month later the Spanish armies totally defeated Francis I at Pavia and took him prisoner, and the French returning from Naples were cut to pieces by the Colonna, resulting virtually in civil war in Rome itself between the Colonna and the Orsini. Although Charles's peace terms looked moderate, despite colossal indemnities and the surrender of cities as guarantees, he never kept his side of the treaties, and Francis I, a prisoner in Madrid, agreed to all the terms put to him, but broke them all the moment he was back in France again. Clement found himself totally under Spanish domination, and in his endeavours to free himself once again sided with the French, but the French king, weary of his Italian adventures, coldly abandoned Clement, and in September 1526 the Colonna attacked Rome and sacked the Vatican. The papal armies in the north of Italy, under the command of the Duke of Urbino, remained totally inactive, and in desperation Clement once again tried to negotiate with Charles V, but by this time the Constable of Bourbon, general of the Imperial forces, had begun a descent into Italy at the head of a partly Spanish but mainly Lutheran army raised for the express purpose of conquering Italy and destroying Rome and the papacy. Clement succeeded in making terms with Bourbon's second-in-command in January, but Bourbon refused to ratify the terms as his rabble was totally out of control, unpaid, starving, shoeless in a bitter winter, mutinous and determined on the plunder of Florence and Rome. They were deflected from Florence by the timely arrival of Urbino and his forces, and on 5 May they were encamped outside Rome which was virtually undefended. The assault started on 6 May in thick fog. Bourbon was killed; Clement took refuge in the Castel S. Angelo; and the sack of the city started. The initial phase of the Sack of Rome lasted six weeks, during which time the city was ruthlessly plundered and three-fifths of it burnt, the inhabitants murdered and tortured to reveal their wealth, the churches totally despoiled, and the Vatican given over to pillage. Eventually, the consequences of the Sack made themselves felt even to the conquerors: the plundering rabble had money and booty beyond its wildest dreams, but there was no food, no fuel except by the demolition of houses, and finally the vast number of rotting corpses in the summer heat resulted in plague following on the heels of famine. The pope remained a prisoner in the Castel S. Angelo, and though some of the soldiery retreated northwards, sacking Narni on the way, a large number remained in Rome as a 'garrison'. The fate of Rome and the pope shocked Christendom, was greeted with expressions of horror and disgust in Spain, and alienated the friends and supporters of Charles V, for despite his disclaimers he was blamed for Bourbon's action. A second phase of the Sack came in September, when the retreating Germans returned to the city to demand more money, and it was not until December that the Imperial forces finally left the Castel S. Angelo, and Clement, with the connivance of his captors, escaped to Orvieto. Even there, conditions were frightful, for though he was free, he had lost all his territories, treasures, subjects, and was abjectly poor. Food was at famine prices, and there was no possibility of breaking out of Orvieto because all the surrounding countryside was infested with German *landsknechts*. Despite his terrible fate, the pope was still courted as a power by both the French and the Imperialists, who regarded him as a moral force and sought to further their political ends by the manipulation of his spiritual role.

The position in Florence during these last years had been confused and unhappy. When Clement became pope, and had to give up governing Florence himself, he dispatched to the city two young Medici bastards – Ippolito, son of Giuliano of Nemours, and Alessandro, son of Lorenzo of Urbino by a mulatto slavewoman. With them he sent Cardinal Passerini as governor in their name; a bad choice, since the cardinal was universally detested. Medici control lasted until the Sack of Rome, but immediately after it the two youths and their mentor prudently retired from Florence, the republican constitution elaborated after the first Medici expulsion in 1494 was restored, and on 31 May 1527 the Grand Council elected Niccolò Capponi as Gonfalonier. Unfortunately, popular opinion in Florence still remained pro-French and despite Capponi's efforts to conclude a satisfactory treaty with the Spaniards, Florence decided to contribute men and money to the French cause. But after the total defeat of the French before Naples, and the conclusion of peace between Charles V and Clement, the decision was taken to restore the Medici control of Florence once again. Capponi was displaced as Gonfalonier, when his secret negotiations with Clement were discovered, and the new man in control, Francesco Carducci, was determined that the city should not surrender its newly regained liberties without a blow. Michelangelo was employed to rebuild the fortifications, for which many of his drawings exist, and during the summer he visited Ferrara *134* to study the famous fortifications there (another result of this visit was the cartoon for a *Leda*, commissioned by the duke, but never delivered). But in September 1529 suspicion of impending treachery caused him to take sudden flight to Venice, although on being pardoned for his action and besought to return and help, he returned by mid-October, and his system of fortifications was so successful that it proved impossible to take Florence by assault. The forces under the Prince of Orange, therefore, reduced the city by siege, despite the brave attempts of Francesco Ferruccio to maintain a life-line for supplies from outside. Malatesta Baglioni, the Perugian employed by the Florentines as their military commander, foreseeing the inevitable end once the stranglehold of the besiegers brought the city to famine, opened secret negotiations with the Prince of Orange, and after both Orange and Ferruccio had been killed, a change of government in Florence facilitated the eventual surrender, which took place in August 1530. The peace treaty called for no reprisals, but this was disregarded, and Carducci and several other members of the government were beheaded. A determined search was made for Michelangelo, who went into hiding. A very interesting discovery recently made of drawings which can be attributed to him on the walls of the crypt under the altar space and the *lavamani* of the Medici Chapel make it clear that his hiding-place was here, and that he must, from datable incidents, have been concealed in the chapel, probably with the help of Figiovanni, for some two months. In October Clement wrote pardoning his activities during the siege, and requiring him to continue working on the Medici tombs and the Laurenziana. This the artist did, but his heart was no longer in the work; moreover, he lived in fear of the hatred of the newly imposed Medici ruler, the degenerate Alessandro.

In the autumn of 1533, Clement VII agreed to meet Francis I at Nice, to conclude the marriage of Catherine de' Medici with the second son of the King of France (later Henri II). On the way he stopped at S. Miniato al Tedesco, just south-west of Empoli, and there saw Michelangelo for the last time. It must have been at this moment that the question of the altar wall in the Sistine Chapel was first broached, and there is good evidence that the first idea was for a *Resurrection*. In October, Michelangelo was in Rome, making the first sketches for the new work, and also continuing work on the Julius Tomb. He returned to Florence for three months in the summer of 1534, when his father died, during which time he also worked on the Laurenziana, and in August 1534 he left Florence for good.

CHAPTER FOUR

The Last Judgment. The Presentation Drawings. The Completion of the Julius Tomb. The Cappella Paolina

When, about 1512, Julius II had finally succeeded in his campaigns to recover control of the papal domains, he considered a suitable commemoration. Despite the dedication of the Sistine Chapel to the Assumption, his first idea was for a new altarpiece representing the Resurrection – 'Resurgam' almost as a cry of personal triumph – and for this Michelangelo prepared one of his most beautiful drawings. Whether it was the nudity of the *Risen Christ* that put the pope off, or whether he changed his mind so as not to conflict with the existing dedication, the project was abandoned and instead his successes were commemorated in Raphael's Stanza d'Eliodoro, which is dedicated to Divine intervention in favour of the Church. In particular, the fresco of the *Deliverance of St Peter* is exactly in the context of this moment of history. Michelangelo's anger at the loss of this commission is reflected in the first of his sonnets, in which he upbraids Julius for the mortification inflicted on him; it also probably still further fuelled his dislike of Raphael. Other designs for a *Resurrection* formed part of the S. Lorenzo façade project, probably as a relief over the door, and a drawing possibly made in connection with the Julius Tomb was adapted in 1516 by Sebastiano del Piombo for the *Raising of Lazarus* (London, National Gallery), for which Michelangelo provided help in the form of drawings. Further treatments of the subject were prepared for the lunettes of the Medici Chapel, some of them distinctly reminiscent of the crucified *Haman* in the Sistine Ceiling lunette, and a drawing of the *Risen Christ* is on the wall of the crypt in which Michelangelo hid during the dangerous days after the fall of Florence in 1531, so that he was still planning future work in the chapel even while he was in hiding from the agents of the Medici family.

110

In 1525, draperies at the back of the altar of the Sistine Chapel caught fire, and Perugino's altarpiece of the *Assumption* was apparently damaged. Nothing was done at the time, but when Clement VII returned to Rome after the terrors and devastations of the Sack, the idea of a new altarpiece was revived; indeed, the vandalism perpetrated in the Vatican may well have made it essential. The subject of the Resurrection was not only historically as

110 MICHELANGELO Drawing for a *Resurrection* 1512

apposite for Clement as it had been for Julius, but it also completed the sequence of thought of the rest of the decoration of the chapel, in that the Creation as the first act of the Old Testament is complemented by the Resurrection as the final act of the New Testament, and the Fall of Man and the degradation of humanity under the Old Dispensation leads to the Redemption under the New Dispensation. It continues that alternation and contrast of the world *ante legem, sub lege* and *sub gratia* which is the theme of the Ceiling and the earlier fresco cycles of the Lives of Moses and Christ on the walls. There had been a *Resurrection* at the end of the earlier Christ cycle, but it was badly damaged in 1522 when part of the doorway into the chapel collapsed. The first projects for Michelangelo's work on the altar wall also involved a replacement of the ruined *Resurrection* with a 'Fall of the Rebel Angels', but the scheme was abandoned, and the present two poor works which complete the 1481 cycles were done by two nonentities after Michelangelo's death. (In fact, some of the ideas present in the *Last Judgment* in the fall of the damned to Hell may well reflect forms which had their inception in the project for the Rebel Angels.)

But the Sistine Chapel project resulted in further complications over the Julius Tomb. The 1516 contract involved only half the number of figures proposed in 1512, and in order to continue with the Tomb while working in Florence, Michelangelo had had the statues and marbles sent there. But work

111 MICHELANGELO Drawing for a *Resurrection* c. 1525/30

112 MICHELANGELO Drawing for a *Resurrection* 1532/33

on the Medici Chapel meant that very little was done, and in 1531 after the siege the Duke of Urbino, unwilling – or unable – to spend more money on the Tomb, cancelled the 1516 contract. Several proposals were made concerning the fate of the unfinished work: Michelangelo could send all the materials and statues in Florence back to Rome and have the Tomb completed by other artists; the artist himself offered to cancel the whole contract and refund the moneys he had received. But Pope Clement, realizing that this would make Michelangelo profoundly unhappy, urged him to complete the Tomb. In April 1532 he came to Rome and signed a new contract, which provided for the erection of the Tomb in S. Pietro in Vincoli, Julius II's titular church as cardinal. Clement, who wanted the new (1533) project in the Sistine Chapel started as soon as possible, undertook to allow him about two months in each year to work on the Tomb, and Michelangelo agreed to provide a new model and to include six of the unfinished figures. He hired an assistant, and while he was working on the Sistine project he secretly went on with the Tomb (which might account for some of the delays in starting on the fresco), but after the death of Clement in 1534 Paul III refused to allow him to continue working on anything but his own projects. The Tomb, therefore, hung fire for a further ten years.

For the altar wall, Michelangelo prepared drawings which expressed the theme of the Resurrection in a totally new way. Instead of the traditional arrangement in which Christ steps out of the sepulchre or thrusts His way out from beneath its rising lid, Christ floats effortlessly from the open tomb, soaring above the bodies of the guards who fall back stricken in terror and wonder.

111, 112

Scaffolding was erected in the Sistine Chapel in March 1534, presumably for the preparation of the wall; in September Clement died suddenly. After a two-day Conclave Alessandro Farnese was elected as Paul III on 13 October. At this point the records are unclear, and the various writers contradictory. Some maintain that the change to a *Last Judgment* was made by Clement VII; others that the new pope changed the subject. Certainly in November 1536 Paul III issued a brief to the effect that Michelangelo should paint according to the cartoons prepared for Clement.

A new scaffolding was erected by April 1535 – which implies either that the original one was removed for the Conclave, or that changes in the project made the earlier one inadequate – the string-courses and cornices were removed, and the two windows blocked up (there is some argument whether these windows were real ones or merely fictive windows like those on the entrance wall; the direction of lighting in the Moses and Christ cycles, and on the figures in the Ceiling, particularly the prophets and sibyls, indicates that they were real windows). The frescoes at the beginning of the Moses and Christ cycles (the *Finding of Moses* and the *Nativity*), the altarpiece, and some of the Ancestors of Christ which Michelangelo himself had painted in the two lunettes, were all destroyed and the whole wall became the field for the painter's apocalyptic vision. The area to be covered was the largest that ever an artist had faced: it is now some 45 ft by 40 ft (13.7 m by 12.2 m). In having the surface prepared, Michelangelo arranged that the actual wall should be cut back so that the wall had an overhang which originally amounted to about 14 in (35 cm), but now, because of mutilations at the base of the fresco, amounts to about 11 in (28 cm). This was to avoid the commonest cause of damage to frescoes: the accumulation of dust on the surface.

On 1 September 1535 Paul III appointed Michelangelo to be his principal painter, sculptor and architect (this last point is important, since Sangallo was still alive and active on projects for St Peter's). The appointment was made to forestall trouble with the Duke of Urbino, who was clamouring for the completion of the Julius Tomb. When Michelangelo had objected to the commission for the *Last Judgment* on the grounds of his commitment to the contract for the Tomb, the pope in a fury declared that he had waited for thirty years to be able to employ Michelangelo and that now that the moment when his ambition was to be realized had come he would tear up the contract if any objections were made. The duke consented that Michelangelo should suspend work on the Tomb for the duration of work on the *Last Judgment*. The cartoon for the *Last Judgment* was apparently ready by September 1535, though this was probably only a *modello* of the whole, and not the working cartoons which were almost certainly destroyed by the painter during the execution of the work. Sebastiano del Piombo, who was in charge of preparing the wall, persuaded the pope that oil was the best medium for so large a work, and had the wall prepared for oil-painting, but Michelangelo, later remarking that oil-painting was fit only for women and lazy people like Sebastiano, had the surface hammered off and redone for true fresco. This was done by January 1536, and work started between 10 April and 18 May 1536. In January 1537 Paul III was urging Michelangelo to hasten the work; on 4 February 1537 he came to see what progress had been made. In September 1537 Michelangelo received a letter from Aretino making suggestions about what he should represent in the work, to which the painter answered coldly that his work was now virtually finished – which was untrue, but understandable. When, in January 1538, Aretino wrote asking for a sketch or part of the cartoon Michelangelo made no answer. Part of the fresco may have been visible when the scaffolding was lowered some time before 15 December 1540 (when the carpenter was paid for his work); the celebrated incident which Vasari and others record about Biagio da Cesena, probably occurred soon after this. The officious papal Master of Ceremonies had apparently got a sight of the fresco, despite Michelangelo's known objections to his work being seen when only partly finished, and complained to the pope about the nude figures in it which he dubbed obscene. In revenge, Michelangelo portrayed him as Minos, Prince of Hell, and when Cesena protested to the pope and demanded that Michelangelo should be made to alter the figure, Paul replied that he had dominion in Heaven and Earth, but that his writ did not run in Hell. The incident, amusing as it is, would not be significant were it not for the fact that it is the first hint of coming trouble, trouble which became far more serious as time brought changes in the attitudes of later popes, and in the approach to the arts during the Counter-Reformation. The fresco was finally unveiled on 31 October 1541, exactly twenty-nine years after the unveiling of the Ceiling. The story goes that when Paul III first saw the fresco in its entirety, he gazed at it awestruck and then fell on his knees beseeching God not to remember his sins on the Day of Judgment.

114 Time, dirt, restoration, and deliberate damage have all played havoc with the work. The contrast between the limpid colour of the Ceiling and the turgid and harsh tones of the huge wall fresco is particularly striking, although the gloomy tonalities of the Ancestors of Christ form a transition to the starker colours of the *Last Judgment* where the background of sky is in streaky blue-grey, and the bodies in varying tones of brown. The iconography is still traditional; while Michelangelo has adhered to the accepted treatment of the scene, it is in his handling of certain details and in the sweep of his imaginative conception of the whole that the revolutionary aspect of the fresco is most striking. The great precursors are the mosaic on the end wall of the cathedral in Torcello, which Michelangelo might have seen on one of his two visits to Venice; the Giotto *Last Judgment* in the Arena Chapel in Padua, which there is no certainty that he ever saw; the Cavallini in S. Cecilia in Rome, now badly mutilated, but which he would have known in its entirety; the four renderings of the scene in the Pisani pulpits in Pisa, Siena and Pistoia; the Nardo di Cione in Sta Maria Novella in Florence; the Traini in the Campo Santo at Pisa; and, most influential of all, the *113* impressive Signorelli in the cathedral at Orvieto. The Last Judgment was not a very popular subject, and though there are other examples, these are the most important ones. Only the Signorelli has the main scene of judgment on an altar wall: all the other painted versions are on entrance walls, while the Traini is in a cloister. Nearly all have a figure of Christ which is clothed, bearded and mild in character; only the Orvieto Christ (which is by Fra Angelico, Signorelli's forerunner in the commission) has the minatory gesture of the right arm raised in rejection and condemnation. Other traditional features in Michelangelo's work are the blessed on Christ's right-hand side, and the damned on His left, while from the Signorelli Michelangelo has taken the two new ideas of the dead rising from the ground with their bare bones being clothed with flesh as they do so, and the entirely human quality of the devils who torment the damned. Also, like Signorelli, he has adopted the nudity of the blessed and the damned, since the notion of the dead emerging from their graves fully clothed must have struck both artists as irrational, it not ridiculous. There the resemblances end.

113 Luca Signorelli *The Last Judgment: The Damned* 1500–04

Michelangelo's treatment of the scene is full of movement; with the exception of the Signorelli, all the other treatments are static, even though they contain plenty of expressive gesticulation. The Signorelli scenes of the *Resurrection* and the blessed in *Paradise* are calmness itself: the trumpeting angels evoke only mild surprise; the blessed stand around with expressions of placid thankfulness while a choir of angels makes music overhead. Only the damned in their ghastly battle with energetic demons form a compact, struggling, terrified mass of bodies, seething in desperate fear and horror.

In the Michelangelo *Last Judgment* there is a huge circulating movement; the figures emerge from the left at the trumpeting of the summoning angels in the middle, and rise towards the menacing figure of Christ in Judgment in the centre, and then fall away into the damned in Hell on the right, where Charon drives them forward from his barque with savage blows of his oar. *114* *115* *116* *118*

In the centre of the fresco, at the bottom, immediately behind the altar, is the mouth of Hell itself, and the imagery of Salvation is completed by the Cross on the altar: the Cross of the Redeemer alone stands between Mankind and *116* Hell. The minatory figure of Christ is surrounded by the saints who have *117* suffered for His sake, holding the instruments of their martyrdom and clamouring for the reward of their faith against the impious, the unjust, the wrongdoers. Huge and threatening, they cry for justice while below them the sinners fall headlong to their doom. In the two lunettes at the top of the fresco are athletic angels carrying the instruments of Christ's Passion, as vivid reminders of the Sacrifice which the sinners have rejected. No one here is tormented by fantastic demons in grotesque mixtures of animal and human: the devils are human in form and Man is not dragged to punishment without being able to understand the cause of his damnation. The consciousness of his own acts, the realization – too late – that he is the sole author of his own disaster, is the most poignant, the most terrifying lesson that Michelangelo's vision of Hell forces upon the spectator, and is tragically exemplified by the *118* horrified face of the despairing man carried off by the demon, and the *115* wondering apprehension in the expression of the skeletal figure emerging from the ground. The echoes of the *Dies Irae* thunder through this apocalyptic vision, with the passionate and fearful urgings of the Requiem Mass: 'Eternal light shine upon them, Lord, with Thy saints for ever, for Thou art merciful . . .'

The forms Michelangelo has used for his figures show the changes which have taken place in his conception of the human body. No longer are his nudes the graceful, lithe, youthful figures of the Ceiling, the *Dying Slave* or the *Victory*. They are massive, thickset, with bulging muscles and sinewy *116* limbs. His beardless Christ is as much a Jupiter Tonans as the Saviour; Mary cowers behind Him, shrinking beneath His upraised arm in recognition that the moment for intercession is now past, and averting her eyes from the *117* tragedies enacted below her. The saints clustering round the avenging Christ are ungainly figures, some sprawled on rock-like clouds, others shambling forward in clamorous urgency. There is no perspective in that each group, each figure even, is seen in its own space, and the effect which photographs emphasize of the larger figures at the top of the fresco, with smaller figures in the lower part, is not so noticeable when standing before the actual painting, since the natural perspective of the diminution of things further away from the point of vision counterbalances Michelangelo's treatment of scale – as he must have intended that it should.

The later history of the fresco is tragic: Michelangelo's self-portrait in the flayed skin of St Bartholomew was indeed prophetic. Paul III was an open-minded pontiff, with an understanding of art, but constantly during his reign

114 MICHELANGELO *The Last Judgment* 1534–41

voices were raised against the nudes of which the *Last Judgment* is almost entirely composed. Even close friends of Michelangelo joined in the condemnation. The artist had been accustomed, from soon after his return to Rome, to meet friends for discussions on religion and faith; these were matters of passionate argument in the years when Lutheranism propagated new doctrines – notably that of salvation through faith alone, a doctrine derived from the Pauline Epistles – and the reform of the Church was a major concern. He met Vittoria Colonna probably for the first time in 1536; she was in Rome from 1538 to 1541, and again from 1544 to her death in 1547. She was a member of this group of friends, which included the Dominican Ambrogio Politi, known as 'Il Caterino', and the so-called 'spiritual' Cardinals: Contarini, the English Cardinal Pole, and the formidable Carafa, who later became Paul IV. Caterino was a dedicated heresy-hunter and for him Michelangelo's *Last Judgment* was suspect because he simply equated any divergence from tradition or from decorum as tending towards irreligion and therefore heresy. Another like-minded cleric was Bernardino Cirillo, who claimed that the degeneration of church music could be likened to the licences of the *Last Judgment*. Despite continual sniping nothing happened during the remainder of Paul III's reign, although by the end of his life the pope was so undermined by the opposition to the fresco that he was said to be considering having it destroyed. Perhaps it may have been because of this bitter polemic that Titian, when he was in Rome in 1545–46, said in front of the work, 'O evil fate, if Time were to damage or destroy this too!'

A major attack was launched by the disreputable Aretino in a letter written to Michelangelo in 1545, in which he virulently attacked the depiction of '. . . saints and angels, the former without any of the decency proper to this world, and the latter lacking any of the loveliness of Heaven', and further castigated the exposure of 'genitals and organs of those in ecstasy in such relief that even in the whore-houses they couldn't fail to make one close one's eyes'. He accused Michelangelo of betraying decorum and of desecrating the major chapel of Christendom merely to gratify his art by painting figures '. . . more permissible on the walls of a voluptuous brothel than on the walls of a choir . . .', and ends his diatribe with the unctuous remark that it were better to displease the artist, whom in the same breath he calls 'our immortal intellect', by 'speaking . . . than to offend Christ by keeping silent'. Michelangelo made no answer; unwilling to waste a potentially valuable letter, Aretino addressed a version of it to a Roman friend so as to ensure its publication. This second version has been dated 1547, but a mention of 'the new Pontiff' can only refer to Julius III, so that the second version must be after February 1550, and probably close in date to

115 MICHELANGELO *The Last Judgment* (detail)

116 MICHELANGELO *The Last Judgment* (detail)

117 MICHELANGELO *The Last Judgment* (detail)

the publication in the spring of 1550 of Vasari's first edition of his famous *Lives*, which contained the first biography of Michelangelo, and a long and enthusiastic eulogy of the *Last Judgment*. Though Aretino's criticism is particularly distasteful, coming from the kind of man he was, its malevolence is matched by the accuracy with which he felt the pulse of clerical – and perhaps also of public – feeling in Italy. The splendid days of artistic liberty were over; the artist was now to be hedged about with rules of decorum that precluded the nude in religious works unless there was no alternative: the Crucifixion, and certain martyrdoms would not make sense if the nude were totally forbidden. But many formerly popular scenes were now rejected on the grounds either that the Gospels provided no evidence for them, or that they formed part of an apocryphal account, or even that the incident was now discredited. Even in mythologies the representation of the nude became less overt, more discreet, with Diana in a hunting tunic and Venus veiled.

Julius III died in 1555, and Marcellus II died twenty-two days after his election, to be followed by the Theatine Cardinal Carafa, Paul IV, who had been one of the bitterest critics of the *Last Judgment* from the time of its unveiling. On his election, he sent word to Michelangelo that he was to 'make it suitable', provoking the devastating reply: 'Tell the pope that this is a small matter and it can easily be made suitable; let him make the world a suitable place and painting will soon follow suit.' Notwithstanding his dislike of the fresco, the pope did nothing about it. Michelangelo during these years was deeply involved in the building of St Peter's, and Paul IV may well have felt that it was hardly appropriate to employ Michelangelo on so important a work, for which he refused all payment, while mutilating one of the painter's major masterpieces. But the polemic continued, and it provided one of the arguments in the debate and influenced the decrees which emanated from the last session of the Council of Trent in December 1563 on the type of art to be permitted in churches.

The 'reform' of the *Last Judgment* was one of thirty-three decrees placed, under the heading 'urgent', before Cardinal Carlo Borromeo, the nephew of Pius IV, immediately the Council closed, and the decision to repaint part of the fresco was taken on 21 January 1564 by a commission headed by Michelangelo's friend, Cardinal Morone, a strict Theatine. Michelangelo died on 18 February 1564: he therefore knew what was intended, although the opponents of his great work at least had the decency to stay their hand during his lifetime. The commission employed for this ungrateful task Daniele da Volterra, who had always been one of Michelangelo's most fervent admirers; he claimed that he had only used *fresco secco* (a form of painting in distemper which is removable), but it is clear that for the St

118 MICHELANGELO *The Last Judgment* (detail)

119 MICHELANGELO *Divine Head* 1532/34?

Catherine, one of the most abused figures, he in fact hacked the original *intonaco* from the wall, and his repainting was drastic, and bad, in the extreme. Several other men – contemptuously described as the 'breeches-makers' – were employed during successive pontificates until the time of Sixtus V on the work of providing Michelangelo's figures with loincloths and other draperies, and it was only with difficulty that a representative from the artists of the Accademia di S. Luca persuaded Clement VIII, pope from 1592 to 1605, that the destruction which he contemplated would be a monstrous crime against Christian civilization, and one that would incur lasting blame. Nor must El Greco's outburst in 1575 be forgotten, when he said that if the pope (then Gregory XIII) were to destroy the fresco he could paint another *Last Judgment* as good and more suitable, a remark which, coming from a foreigner, did little to endear him to Roman artists.

Michelangelo's friendship with Vittoria Colonna gave rise to several magnificent drawings. The making of these 'presentation drawings' goes back to the early days of his return to Rome and to his friendship with

120 MICHELANGELO *Divine Head*
1532/34?

Tommaso Cavalieri. During the summer of 1532, when he was in Rome working on a new phase of the Julius Tomb, he first met Cavalieri, a young Roman of good family (he served for years in an official civic capacity as a Conservatore). The young man was of supreme beauty, as all his contemporaries admitted, and Michelangelo, always an admirer of male beauty – most of his female figures, as is known from the Sistine Ceiling drawings, were made from male figures and merely converted into women – was deeply affected by him. While their correspondence preserves the high-flown tone of extravagant literary language customary at the time, and some of Michelangelo's sonnets addressed to the young man might suggest a less exalted relationship, the elderly artist (Michelangelo was then fifty-seven, and Cavalieri probably in his early twenties) insists that their love was Platonic and that he was well aware of the barriers which religion and social custom placed between them and any irregular association. The friendship endured, for Cavalieri was present at Michelangelo's death and inherited many of his drawings, some of which, unfortunately, he failed to preserve.

121 MICHELANGELO *The Punishment of Tityus* 1532

For Cavalieri, Michelangelo made a group of drawings of classical subjects which were apparently designed to help the young man to learn to draw, and Vasari says that several drawings of heads in black and red chalk were also done for the same purpose. These are the very beautiful so-called 'Teste Divine' – Divine Heads – representing types of beauty drawn from the artist's imagination rather than from any living models. One of Michelangelo's few portrait drawings is recorded as having been made of Cavalieri, a full-length life-size drawing which has not survived (the only known portrait drawing is a beautiful one of the young Florentine Andrea Quaratesi, done in 1532). The group of classical drawings includes a *Tityus*, a *Ganymede*, a *Fall of Phaethon*, a so-called *Children's Bacchanal*, and two other drawings of which the meaning is obscure: the *Archers* and the *Dream of Human Life*. The choice of the recognizable classical subjects is curiously indicative. The myth of Tityus, condemned for an assault upon the goddess Leto to have his liver, believed to be the seat of the passions, eternally consumed by two eagles and eternally renewed so as to perpetuate the torment, is a symbol of the punishment of illicit passion. The myth of Ganymede, snatched up to Olympus by Zeus' eagle to become the god's cup-bearer, is a symbol of the aspiration of the soul to higher, nobler things. The myth of Phaethon, who so mismanaged the chariot of the Sun which his father Helios had unwillingly allowed him to drive that Zeus, to save the Heavens and Earth from destruction, killed him with a thunderbolt, while his

119, 120

121

122

sisters who bewailed his fate were turned into poplar trees and his brother Cygnus into a swan, is a symbol of the punishment of *hubris* – improper and vainglorious pride – but may well in this context be a symbol of the fate of one who aims at what is beyond him. The figures in these compositions, particularly in the three known versions of the *Phaethon*, reflect forms which Michelangelo had used in the Sistine Ceiling and the Medici tombs. It is interesting to note, however, that one of the drawings on the walls of the crypt in which he lay hidden after the siege of Florence is a *Fall of Phaethon* which the Cavalieri drawings closely resemble, so that the subject must have been in his mind in quite another context as early as 1530. It is also noteworthy that his mastery of the human form is not paralleled by any mastery of the forms of horses. The resemblance between the figure of Zeus

122 MICHELANGELO *The Fall of Phaethon* 1533

123 MICHELANGELO *Children's Bacchanal* 1533?

124 MICHELANGELO *Archers shooting at a Herm* 1533?

125 MICHELANGELO *The Dream of Human Life* 1533/34?

hurling his thunderbolt and the Christ of the *Last Judgment* is interesting as showing the way in which one work leads into another, one train of thought is continued in another context. *116*

The meaning of the *Children's Bacchanal* has never been elucidated: the gloomy and anxious appearance of all the figures belies the title and suggests a meaning along the lines of the oppressiveness of earthly and material cares. The *Archers* aim their arrows at a target suspended on a herm, yet they hold no bows, and the only figure that does is bending it to fix its cord. Do the arrows represent 'the arrows of desire', which reach their target only to destroy it? The *Dream of Human Life* is equally enigmatic: Fame awakens the Dreamer with his trumpet-call; the Dreamer sits on a box which contains the masks of illusion and leans upon the globe of the world. Around the Dreamer circulate the images of the deadly sins, from which Pride alone is missing. Does he represent Pride, claiming the world for his own and *123* *124* *125*

126 Michelangelo
Crucifixion c. 1540

holding in reserve the illusions with which Mankind is deceived? Does Fame persuade the awakening Dreamer that glory may be his, despite the temptations with which he is surrounded?

The classical subjects may have been chosen because Cavalieri preferred them – he later formed a notable collection of classical antiquities – but they are equally suited to the curiously ambivalent relationship between himself and the artist. In technique, the drawings form a strong contrast to Michelangelo's normally purposeful draughtsmanship; there is none of his usual searching out of contour in repeated outlines, no development of form through cross-hatching, or passages left unfinished when further study of a form became unnecessary. They are executed in an extraordinarily painstaking and detailed manner, by stippling the chalk so that the forms emerge in *chiaroscuro* as if breathed upon the paper – a cold, almost feelingless technique which may well have been designed for the didactic purpose assigned to them, since a number of copies exist. (The Quaratesi portrait drawing is in the same technique and was done before Michelangelo left Florence in 1534.)

The drawings made for Vittoria Colonna are exclusively of religious subjects, as befitted so pious a woman. By birth a Colonna, and a granddaughter of Federigo da Montefeltro, she was the widow of the Marquis of Pescara, who fought in the Spanish army against the French and died of the wounds he suffered at the Battle of Pavia in 1525. After her husband's death she devoted herself to a spiritual life, joining the circle of reformers round Cardinals Pole and Carafa, and became celebrated for her deep piety and nobility of mind. Michelangelo's drawings for her include a superb *Crucifixion*, and a *Pietà* with the Virgin supporting the dead Christ between her knees at the foot of the Cross. In this last drawing the Cross itself bears the strange and enigmatic inscription taken from Dante's

126

127

127 Michelangelo *Pietà* 1538/40

128 MICHELANGELO *Holy Family (Madonna of Silence)* 1540?

Paradiso: 'Non vi si pensa quanto sangue costa' ('You little think how much blood costs' or 'You little think how much blood it costs'). A *Holy Family*, known as the *Madonna of Silence* from the gesture of the young Baptist, probably also belongs to this group, all the drawings being in the delicate stippled technique which was used for the Cavalieri drawings. When Vittoria died in 1547 Michelangelo was distraught, and in a letter to a friend referred to himself as being 'beside oneself with grief'. For him, she must have represented the other pole from the love of physical beauty which Cavalieri represented, and her early death reinforced his own ever-growing piety, his natural pessimism, and his concern with death. Some of his drawings suggest that he may have planned a monument to her in the form of a Crucifixion with the Virgin and St John at the foot of the Cross, since one drawing is of detailed dimensions for marble blocks sufficient for life-sized figures, and several others are variants on the theme of the Crucifixion.

128

129 MICHELANGELO *Brutus* *c.* 1540

During the time that Michelangelo was working on the *Last Judgment* he began the bust of *Brutus*, which apparently resulted from his connection with Florentine exiles in Rome after the restoration of the Medici. In 1537, Lorenzino murdered his cousin Alessandro, and this tyrannicide was equated in anti-Medicean circles with the action of Brutus in killing Caesar. According to Vasari, the bust was suggested to Michelangelo by Donato Giannotti, who had been among the defenders of Florence during the siege, and who was now in the service of Cardinal Niccolò Ridolfi, another ardent anti-Medicean. After Michelangelo's death, the bust was acquired by Grand Duke Francesco de' Medici and an inscription was placed on it to the effect that Michelangelo had abandoned the work on realizing that he was commemorating a murder. Whether this inscription tells the truth or was just a piece of Medici propaganda it is now impossible to know, but Michelangelo left the bust unfinished and kept it, since he gave it to Tiberio

129

Calcagni, who was not born until 1532 and did not enter Michelangelo's circle until the mid-1550s. Calcagni worked over the draperies using a flat chisel, whereas Michelangelo's own work was done with a claw chisel. The bust was inspired by Roman Imperial busts, of which there were many versions in Rome. From the front, the profile is powerful and noble, but seen from the side, full-face, it is gross and heavy with a thick bull-neck. This curiously ambivalent quality may be intentional, or just a result of its unfinished state.

Once the *Last Judgment* was finished, Michelangelo was faced with the completion of the Julius Tomb. Paul III had already decided on the decoration of the Cappella Paolina in the Vatican, so that another – and this time final – contract was drawn up in 1542 which only required that Michelangelo should supply three statues from his own hand for the Tomb. As a result of an adroit comment by a member of the pope's entourage when Paul visited Michelangelo's studio, it was decided that the *Moses* would suffice; the two *Slaves*, completed in 1516, were probably originally the other two statues. But the reduced size of the final project meant that the two *Slaves* were now too large for the places designed for them, and the changes in current religious feeling, as well as Michelangelo's own greater spirituality, made them inappropriate, so that he began two figures of *Leah* and *Rachel*, as the Active and Contemplative Life (roles Dante assigned to them in the *Purgatorio*), which were to be placed in the niches on either side of the *Moses*. The *Slaves* were replaced by massive volutes surmounted by herms, and in the upper part of the monument the reclining figure of Pope Julius was to be flanked by a prophet and a sibyl, and a group of the *Madonna and Child* was to be placed in a niche over the recumbent figure of the pope. All these were to be carved by Michelangelo's assistant Raffaello da Montelupo, and Michelangelo was to supervise Raffaello's work – no more. Much of the decorative sculpture on the lower part of the Tomb was left over from the earlier projects and its detailed richness contrasts with the stark and empty forms of the upper part of the monument.

130, 131

The *Rachel* and *Leah* are the last sculptures which Michelangelo completed, but despite their expressive character they have little of the feeling or the quality of form found in his earlier work. Is this because they are clothed and female, where his great strength was in the depiction of the beauty of the nude male? The considerable – wild even – changes of scale as well as variations in skill displayed by the final assemblage of figures render the whole a total justification of Michelangelo's description of it as the 'Tragedy of the Tomb'. No one was happy with the outcome: the della Rovere felt that they had been cheated; Michelangelo that he had been misjudged, unjustly accused of taking money for which he had not supplied

130 MICHELANGELO Tomb of Julius II: *Rachel*

131 MICHELANGELO Tomb of Julius II: *Leah*

132 MICHELANGELO *The Conversion of St Paul* 1542–45

the promised statues, and obliged to settle for a result which had almost nothing in common with the project and the high hopes with which he had started. The final miserable object was unveiled in 1547, in S. Pietro in Vincoli.

81

The Cappella Paolina had been built at a short distance from the Sistine Chapel from about 1537 onwards by Antonio da Sangallo as a private chapel for Paul III. The pope had always intended that Michelangelo should undertake its decoration, the project even antedating the start of work on the *Last Judgment*. He worked on the chapel between 1542 and 1550, while he was finishing the Julius Tomb. While one of the frescoes was always intended to portray the *Conversion of St Paul*, the other was originally planned as a 'Giving of the Keys to Peter', a favourite subject because of the

133 MICHELANGELO *The Crucifixion of St Peter* 1546–50

stress it laid on papal authority; Vasari in his 1550 Life of Michelangelo so described it, but the writing of Vasari's first edition was largely completed about 1546/47. The subject was, however, changed to the *Crucifixion of St Peter*. The work must have been very difficult. Michelangelo was now over seventy, in poor health (he suffered from stones in the bladder), and he complained that he was too old for the hard labour of fresco-painting.

The striking thing about these two frescoes is their colour. They are far closer to the light, clear tonalities of the Ceiling than the heavy, turgid colour of the *Last Judgment* would lead one to expect, and while in the *Conversion* *132* there is a distinction between the earthy colours of the terrestrial part and the more luminous warmth in the Heavenly apparition and the angels

133 surrounding Christ, in the *Crucifixion* the figures surrounding the martyred saint are all warmer and clearer than anything in the *Last Judgment*. There is also a conspicuous restraint in the use of nude figures; only in the *Conversion* are there a few among the angels, mostly seen from the back or else discreetly bowdlerized, and in the *Crucifixion* the only nude is Peter himself.

Other notable features in both frescoes are the circulatory movement and 132 the negation of perspective. In the *Conversion*, the sense of internal space is created by the horse (adapted from the horses of the Dioscuri on the Quirinal Hill) plunging into depth, and by the way the plummeting figure of Christ, off-centre, establishes a line of force in opposition to the movement of the horse and the outstretched body of the blinded Saul. Making the fallen man an old greybeard was probably done in deference to the pope himself; at this moment in the history of Christianity, Saul must have been, if not a young man, then no more than in early middle age, whereas Paul III was, as is known from the portraits by Titian, old and infirm. The *Crucifixion of St* 133 *Peter* has the same curious management of space: a group of half-length figures cut off by the frame stands in distraught horror just within the picture space, while a group of men clambers into the picture suggesting a space beyond the confines of the frame. The horsemen and the lances push into the picture from one side, while another group edges over the brow of the hillock in frightened curiosity to stare at the shocking event happening below. St Peter twists himself round on his cross, raising his massive body on his straining arms, to glare out accusingly at the spectator, while the executioners struggle to heave the cross upwards and towards the hole being dug for it. The whole scene is one of pitiless agony; the spectators are either active in the murderous business, curious, apathetic, or horror-struck, but all turning like a gigantic wheel round the saint at its hub. The *Conversion* took from the end of 1542 until mid-1545, with a long delay in 1544 because Michelangelo was ill; the *Crucifixion* was not begun until 1546, since a fire broke out in the chapel, but caused less damage than was at first believed to the *Conversion* which was already finished. The pope came to see the work in mid-October 1549; he died in November 1549, and the fresco was not finished until 1550. They were Michelangelo's last paintings.

The state of Italy during the pontificate of Paul III was relatively peaceful, which is not surprising since the country was dominated – virtually occupied – by the Spaniards. The petty princes – Ferrara, Mantua, Urbino, Florence – were concerned only with their own preservation, best achieved by wary subservience to the dominant power, and in some cases by military service with it: Ferrante Gonzaga, brother of Duke Federigo of Mantua, was Spain's Governor of Milan and Viceroy of Naples.

Alessandro Farnese came of a noble family from the Bolsena area, north of Rome, and profited by the association of his sister, Giulia Orsini – known as 'La Bella' – with Cardinal Rodrigo Borgia, later Alexander VI, who made him Legate of Ancona. He was so intelligent and capable that he was able to retain the confidence of Julius II, despite his close connection with that pope's detested predecessor. Before he became a priest in 1519 he had several natural children, the chief among them being Pier Luigi and Ranuccio, both of whom were legitimated by Julius II. Pier Luigi became a soldier, Ranuccio a cardinal. After his election in 1534 – one of the speediest ever, Cardinal Farnese being one of the very rare instances of a man breaking the usual rule: 'Who enters the Conclave a pope leaves it a cardinal' – he proved himself a skilful diplomatist in the ever festering quarrels between France and Spain, an excellent ruler and a dedicated churchman. His first concern was the recovery of the Church from the state into which it had fallen after the Sack and the assaults of Lutheranism. The major religious acts of his reign were the recognition of the value of the Jesuits, who between 1538 and 1550 spread over all Europe and as far afield as India, Japan and the Americas, and the summoning of the Council of Trent. His besetting sin was nepotism. In 1545, in the teeth of opposition from the College of Cardinals, he transferred Parma and Piacenza from the Papal States to his unworthy son Pier Luigi, and raised them into a dukedom. Two years later, Pier Luigi was murdered by the contrivance of Ferrante Gonzaga, and a bitter struggle ensued between the dead man's two sons, Ottavio and Orazio, as to who was to succeed to the dukedom. The prolonged family quarrels over the succession finally resulted in the breakdown of the old man's health – he was then eighty-two – and he died on 10 November 1549.

The Conclave which elected his successor was one of the longest and bitterest ever held. Little political pressure had been exerted during the election of Paul III by either Spain or France. Paul III had achieved a policy of neutrality; both the major powers were now determined to control the next pope. The Conclave started on 29 November and lasted until 8 February: nearly eleven weeks of deadlock, which was finally resolved, as such struggles always are eventually, by the election of one of the few neutral men, Cardinal del Monte, as Julius III. The new pope presented the most contradictory qualities. He came of a bourgeois legal family, looked and behaved like a peasant, was so ugly that artists found it difficult to depict him, a great eater, given to sudden attacks of rage, a gambler, a lover of festivities, banquets, music, the theatre, the carnival, and a reckless spender. At the same time he was a dedicated man of business, skilful in statecraft, determined to continue the Council of Trent, to which both Spanish and French kings were opposed, dedicated to the restoration of the Church and its reform. His nepotism was limited to gifts of livings, and money. He was the patron of Palestrina, whom he made director of the choir of St Peter's and a member of the papal choir despite his being a married man. He employed Vignola, Ammanati and Vasari to design and build the superb Villa Giulia on the Via Flaminia to the north of the city. Above all, he was a fervent admirer and supporter of Michelangelo through all the difficulties that beset the ageing artist during the building of St Peter's, and to him Condivi dedicated his *Life of Michelangelo*, published in 1553. His pontificate was short – five years only – and he was succeeded by the harsh Cardinal Pietro Carafa as Paul IV.

The pontificate of Paul IV was mercifully short – lasting from 1555 to 1559 – but very damaging. The pope was seventy-nine at his election, a stern, violent old man, who regarded any slight to his office as an insult to God Himself. His twin ambitions were to restore the Church to what it had been before Luther, and Italy to its state before the 'barbarian' invasions. Unfortunately, he committed the very error he had so condemned in previous popes: he appointed one of his three nephews to supreme political power and made him a cardinal. Carlo Carafa was an appalling choice; venal, grasping, immoral, skilled at hoodwinking his uncle who trusted him completely. Paul IV loathed the Spaniards and indulged the vain hope of expelling them from Italy, even being willing to use the French as allies for the purpose. Eventually, he attacked the Colonna, traditionally allied with Spain, and gave their lands and the title of Duke of Paliano to one of his nephews. In the resulting war with a Spanish army under the Duke of Alba, the pope was utterly defeated.

Finally, Paul's eyes were opened to the true characters and actions of his nephews. He disgraced them completely. He then turned to the reform of the Church, but while pursuing necessary policies against abuses, he used the arm of the Inquisition with increasing harshness, making it a tribunal not only for heresy but for any sin of immorality. He persecuted the Jews, established the Roman ghetto, burnt Jewish books, and followed this with the founding of the Index of Prohibited Books in 1558, heading it with the works of Erasmus. A reign of terror began in Rome, and many people were accused of crimes that brought them within the grasp of that terrible tribunal whose secret trials ended in ghastly public executions or long years in the galleys. The evils of his nephew's misrule, his oppressive taxation, and the disastrous Spanish war boiled over in violence when it was known that the pope was dying. A mob stormed the offices of the Inquisition, freed all the prisoners and burnt the palace, destroying all the records and evidence. It then rushed to the Capitol, where a statue of Paul IV had been erected, and threw it down, dragged it through the streets amid public execration and flung it into the Tiber. A civic decree ordered that all Carafa arms and inscriptions in the city should be removed or defaced, and so violent was popular feeling that the dead pope's body was hurried into a grave in the deepest part under St Peter's and a guard was set over it.

The Conclave that elected Pius IV lasted no less than sixteen weeks, longer even than the bitter battle over the election of Julius III, and for the same reasons. Spanish and French attempts to dominate the choice of the next pope were compounded by the baleful influence of Cardinal Carafa, who was allowed to take part in the Conclave despite the general detestation felt for him. This was because the College of Cardinals would not submit to interference from the civic authorities of Rome, and even less to domination by the populace. Pius IV proved to be an admirable choice. He mitigated most of the harsher decrees of Paul IV, limited the powers of the Inquisition, and made it impossible hereafter for any pope to alienate any part of the Papal States to found principalities for his relatives. Though he had many nephews, the only one who achieved any importance was Cardinal Carlo Borromeo, an admirable prelate whose influence was for the best and who, after his uncle's death, returned to his archbishopric in Milan where his pastoral labours, particularly during the terrible plague of 1576, were such that he was canonized in 1610.

Pius restored good relations with Spain, which had been shattered by Paul IV, and reopened the Council of Trent, bringing it to a successful conclusion in 1563. He dealt with the problem of the Carafa family by bringing the cardinal to trial for his many misdeeds, which included being a party with his brother, the Duke of Paliano, and with her brother and uncle, to the murder of the duchess and the man accused of being her lover. All were executed.

Every pope at his election bound himself to continue building St Peter's. Pius was as active as his financial troubles would allow, giving Michelangelo all the support he needed against the frequent intrigues of place-seekers who went so far as to say that he was senile. Pius also sided with him in the difficulties which he partly created for himself by his alienation of the officials of the Fabbrica – the Office of Works.

134 MICHELANGELO Drawing for the fortifications of Florence 1528/29

CHAPTER FIVE

Michelangelo's Architecture

Michelangelo's earliest architectural commissions are fairly insignificant: a façade for the chapel in Castel S. Angelo about 1514/15, later much altered; the unexecuted design for a gallery round the base of the dome of Florence Cathedral, about 1516/20; what Vasari calls the 'kneeling windows' inserted about 1517 into the formerly open loggia on the corner of the Medici palace in Florence, which set the fashion for pedimented windows borne on volutes. Though the structure of the Julius Tomb could be considered an architectural work, his first real experience of designing part of a building came with the façade for S. Lorenzo (see pp. 108–12), and was followed by the building of the New Sacristy and its interior with the Medici tombs (see pp. 112–25). After this came the Biblioteca Laurenziana (see pp. 125–30), and his other minor commission for S. Lorenzo: the design for the relics loggia, which he planned as a balcony over the inside of the main door. This was commissioned by Clement VII in 1525, and the design was agreed in 1531, but Michelangelo had already left for Rome before it was built.

The fortifications of Florence were built for the defence of the city during the siege of 1528–29. Nothing of them survives on the ground, since they were mainly earthworks with revetments of unbaked brick, and they were later replaced by Antonio da Sangallo with masonry fortifications different from Michelangelo's designs. A number of very interesting drawings exists, *134* showing that the artist considered carefully the defenders' problems of firepower, covering fire and the mobility of artillery, but the complicated silhouettes in the drawings must have been modified by the actual terrain and by the difficulties of construction. In some cases the very complexity of the designs puts them in the category of ideal rather than practical essays in fortress-building. Many of them contain, however, ideas which reappear in seventeenth-century fortification designs, though usually simplified and shorn of their more elaborate and therefore weakening projections.

When the Emperor Charles V visited Rome in 1535 and was escorted through the city with suitable halts for receptions, his party was forced to skirt the Campidoglio – the civic centre of Rome – because there was no road up to it. The temporary decoration of the area was as much to conceal its squalid and dilapidated condition from the illustrious visitor as to do him

135 ITALIAN SCHOOL View of the Capitoline Hill *c.* 1554–60

honour. In 1537 Paul III decided to remove the equestrian statue of Marcus Aurelius from in front of the Lateran to the Campidoglio, and though Michelangelo was opposed to the idea he was asked to design a new pedestal for the statue. This was done in 1538. He sited it in the middle of the area, which was a rough piece of ground bounded on the south by a fifteenth-century arcaded palace, the civic offices of Rome, on the east by the remains of the Roman Tabularium, partly fortified and used as the senate of the city, on the north by the steep retaining wall of the hill crowned by the church of the Aracoeli, and on the west by the scrubby hillside intersected with paths straggling down to the valley below. Fairly soon after, he must have been asked to design a new piazza to become a worthy civic centre for Rome, as distinct from the papal centre of the Vatican, itself haphazard and disorganized as a result of the protracted building operations for the new St Peter's.

135

136

Michelangelo's design marks an epoch in town-planning. He held strong views about symmetry where a central feature dominated, expressing in a letter, unfortunately undated, the view that architecture followed the same rules as the human figure, in that a part one side of a central feature should be

136 Etienne Dupérac Engraving of Michelangelo's design for the Capitoline Hill 1568

mirrored by a matching part as two eyes match on either side of a nose. His design for the new Campidoglio follows these precepts: the Senate-Tabularium was the central feature, and the Conservatori palace on one side had therefore to be matched by a corresponding building on the other side of the piazza (for which there was, at the time, no function); the entrance from the city, up the hillside, was another central feature, and side roads from the Forum at the back and the Tarpeian Rock behind the Conservatori had to be matched by corresponding entrances so as to preserve the symmetry of the whole.

It was the concept of symmetry that was so novel and forward-looking. Many Italian towns have fine civic centres, but only in Vigevano, south of Milan, and to a lesser degree in Venice and Pienza, was the architecture subordinated to a basically scenographic scheme where the whole was more important than the parts. In Vigevano, the late fifteenth-century arcaded houses surround the piazza on three sides, the fourth closed by a church; in Venice, attempts were being made from the late fifteenth century onwards to regularize the Piazza S. Marco, though this was not finally achieved until the end of the sixteenth and early seventeenth century; in Pienza, a deliberate planning of the elements of cathedral, two palaces and town hall round a trapezoidal space had been achieved by Bernardo Rossellino for Pius II between 1459 and 1462, but though the elements are symmetrically sited, they are different in appearance. What was so remarkable about Michelangelo's conception was that he envisaged the Campidoglio as a symmetrical arrangement of similar buildings which would form a fitting open space for public ceremonies: his attitude towards the site was entirely scenographic.

He was reasonable in that he made every allowance for piecemeal construction; Rome was a poor city and the resources of the civic authorities were very straitened. The account books show that work began in the early 1540s and continued until well after Michelangelo's death, since the matching palace to the Conservatori – now the Capitoline Museum – was not begun until 1603 and not finished until the mid-1650s. What is surprising is that the result was so close to Michelangelo's intentions, particularly considering the intervention of Cavalieri and, after Michelangelo's death, of Giacomo della Porta who introduced changes few of which were for the better. The engravings published by Dupérac in 1568 and 1569 do not represent the reality, but the ideal that Michelangelo was aiming at; it is the Conservatori which comes closest to Michelangelo's intentions.

137

136

137 MICHELANGELO Piazza del Campidoglio

138 MICHELANGELO and GIACOMO DELLA PORTA Conservatori Palace, designed before 1546

The Conservatori palace presents several new features. Michelangelo designed it as a façade only; the old building behind it continued in use during the erection of the new front, and, although he probably designed it between 1538 and 1539, and before 1546, since it is unlike the style in which he was working either at the Farnese palace or at St Peter's, work on it was only begun in 1563. Michelangelo's Giant Order runs through the equally proportioned upper and lower floors, so that it becomes the visual support of the massive cornice crowning the whole building. Taken together with the lesser cornice surmounting the minor Order of Ionic columns which supports the entablature of the loggia entrances of the ground floor, these elements form a grid which divides the façade into simple rectangular units. He also uses a device which had already appeared in his Florentine architecture, the layering of surfaces, in that behind the giant pilaster the *138* framework surrounding the bays threads its way down through the lower Order to become part of the pier against which the pedestals of the Giant Order stand. This device became a favourite way for him to enrich the surfaces of his buildings and increase the modulations of light and shadow.

Originally, the windows were designed to be all alike, and they repeat in their use of pedestals, columns and entablature the characteristics of the plain loggia bays below, the only contrast being provided by richly decorated segmental pediments. The huge central window, crammed into the space with difficulty and breaking the over-all rhythm of size and detailing, was one of della Porta's less happy modifications made in 1568; the doubling of the return bay at the end was done in 1660. The interior of the loggia has a richly coffered ceiling, important for later architects such as Palladio. The main structure of the building is in the fine, pale pinkish, thin Roman brick; only the details of the Orders and the windows are in travertine.

137 The Senate offers very little of Michelangelo's work, except for the great staircase – the first of its kind – which was probably begun before 1547 but was not finished until about 1561. In making his design, Michelangelo may well have been inspired by the upper part of the similarly shaped double ramp of Bramante's Belvedere courtyard stairway, but he also had to fit his design to the façade, which his friend Tommaso Cavalieri had designed in 1544 for the Senate, by regularizing the windows on either side of a large doorway, and by putting a new balustrade on a balcony which then ran between the two corner towers. Originally the double flight of this staircase was to have had a portico at the top (truncated bits of the piers are still there), but this was never built. The antique River Gods, which formerly lay in inconvenient abandon in front of the Conservatori, were placed beneath the staircase, and the niche in the centre was filled with a figure of Roma, converted from an antique Minerva, instead of the Jupiter that Michelangelo wanted. Cavalieri's façade had neither the Giant Order nor the layering of the surface by the placing of a pilaster strip behind the pilaster of the Order. These modifications were taken over from the Conservatori palace by della Porta who altered the main *salone* of the Senate in 1573–74; they involved alterations to the façade which were not completed until the 1590s. Della Porta removed the balcony, built out the front, and gave all his windows a much richer decoration. The campanile was originally off-centre; Michelangelo wanted to rebuild it in the middle of the Senate, but this was not done until 1583, when Martino Longhi rebuilt it – it had been destroyed by lightning in 1577. The beautiful paving, with its expanding design, was also altered by della Porta who substituted a dull pattern of diverging rays, but in 1940 the original design by Michelangelo was finally laid.

The causeway, or *cordonata*, down the hillside was planned by

Michelangelo, but built by della Porta who narrowed the ramp towards the bottom. Perhaps the most striking feature of the piazza is its curious trapezoidal shape; the narrowing towards the *cordonata* was the result of the Senate and the Conservatori not being at right angles to each other. Michelangelo brilliantly exploited this imposed condition to create an impression of power funnelled towards the ramp and gushing out to spill down the hillside. The careful placing of the statue of Marcus Aurelius on a slightly domical centre served two purposes, one practical, one symbolic: it drained the rainwater away; it also recalled the old designation of the Campidoglio as the centre of the world – the *caput mundi* – which goes back to the antique tradition of Rome as the *umbilicus mundi* – the navel of the world. In siting the statue to look out across the valley towards the world, Michelangelo emphasized the unique position of ancient Roman power at the hub of the universe: the City's as against the Church's 'Urbi et Orbi'.

Antonio da Sangallo the Younger began the Farnese palace in 1517. *139* Construction continued slowly until Cardinal Alessandro became Pope Paul III in 1534, after which work proceeded more quickly on an enlarged project, but it stopped in the autumn of 1546, when Sangallo died. It appears that at no time was a complete project or design ever made, and the style of the architecture is such that it could be – and was – altered and enlarged at will without compromising the design. At Sangallo's death, the façade had reached the top storey, but despite there being a design for a cornice among his drawings, it was decided to hold a competition for the completion of the façade. Michelangelo's cornice design was chosen before March 1547, since the wooden trial section was in place by then. When Michelangelo took over, he decided to use on the façade the windows Sangallo had designed, but he raised the height of the top storey considerably, so as to improve the visual effect of his huge cornice. He also redesigned the central window, increasing the number of colonnettes, and substituting a flat lintel for Sangallo's arched tops, which made room for the huge coat of arms.

In the courtyard, things were far less advanced. The ground-floor range of *141* Doric arcades was finished, and the parts for the first-floor Ionic Order and arcades were ready, though the much thinner forms of the windows indicate that they, like the infilling of the arcades, were not part of Sangallo's original scheme, but were probably the work of Vignola, who took over from Michelangelo in 1549–50. Michelangelo was able to introduce the rich frieze of swags and masks, and he raised the height between the two floors so as to insert a mezzanine, which in turn meant that his top storey could not continue the arcade theme, since the proportions were now wrong. He resolved the problem by designing an altogether new element with totally anti-classical windows which violated every canon of Vitruvian orthodoxy. *140*

139 ANTONIO DA SANGALLO and MICHELANGELO Farnese Palace, entrance façade

The segmental pediment is detached from the window-frame; the tympanum is broken on either side and decorated by a thin garland suspended from a ram's head; the outer part of the window-frame projects below the inner frame so that, with its lion head and volute decoration, it looks like a pair of flat tassels hanging down over the window. Each window is set into a space bounded by pilasters with his favourite layering device, in this case made not as in the Conservatori by a frame round the area, but by segments of pilasters projecting behind the main one; this enables the main pilaster to preserve something of its correct proportions, while its 'echoes' on either side increase the thickness and, therefore, the effect of the whole member. By setting the pilasters on a thin string-course above the mezzanine, and then by projecting their pedestals into the mezzanine area, he binds the two storeys together while preserving their distinctness. The cornice over the top storey is like no other before or since; the little masks and dentil blocks with tiny guttae below in the lower frieze, and the small florets in the frieze above the entablature, create a scintillating pattern of light and shade. Taken with the window designs, they show his determination not to be bound by any classical precedent and display, as Vasari says, his sense of equality with antiquity and his freedom to design on a par with the ancients.

140 MICHELANGELO Farnese Palace, top-storey window on courtyard

141 MICHELANGELO and GIACOMO VIGNOLA Farnese Palace, courtyard

The rest of Michelangelo's design was never carried out. After the discovery in the Baths of Caracalla of the huge piece of sculpture known as the 'Farnese Bull', which Michelangelo wanted to convert into a fountain and place in the garden, he proposed that a two-storey loggia should be built between the court and the garden, so that there should be a view through from the entrance vestibule into the garden, past the statue-fountain, and across a bridge over the Tiber to another garden on the other side of the river, adjacent to the Farnesina. This would have converted the palace into something far closer to the antique type of *villa suburbana* by combining an urban residence with open vistas of countryside. Instead (because Michelangelo's plan would have involved loss of living rooms) the present less ambitious arrangement was adopted, with a three-bay loggia only on the garden front. Who built this part is uncertain, but it was probably Vignola until his death in 1573; the work was finished in 1589, possibly by della Porta. It was radically altered by rebuilding during the nineteenth century.

When Bramante died in 1514, thirteen months after his great patron Julius II, he left neither complete plans nor finished model for the new St Peter's. His death was the signal for controversy over the problem of central plan versus long nave, and his successors, Giuliano da Sangallo, Fra Giocondo, *142* and Raphael, increased the indecision by making various plans incorporating long naves which destroyed the splendour of Bramante's conception without providing a better solution to the problem of internal space in the basilica. The other great problem, which seems to have been realized at once – probably by Bramante himself – was the size and strength of the piers supporting the dome; every architect who touched the designs enlarged the piers, realizing that the original ones would never bear the weight of a dome of the size projected. After Raphael's death in 1520 (in 1515 Giuliano retired and Fra Giocondo died) Antonio da Sangallo the Younger was appointed architect in charge, with Bramante's erstwhile assistant Peruzzi to help him, but very little indeed was done for the next twenty years, chiefly for lack of *143, 144* money. The spirited drawings which Maerten van Heemskerck made during his stay in Rome in 1532–35 offer the best guide to the state of the basilica at that date.

145 Sangallo had a model made of his new project: a huge affair which cost a fortune and took seven years to build (1539–46). It was a compromise between two shapes: the central plan, which he retained for the main body of the church, and a narthex with a domed section joining it to the central plan as a compromise with the proposals for the long nave. The building was carried quite a way forward on the basis of his model between 1543 and his death in 1546. When Michelangelo was approached to take over responsibility for St Peter's he was very reluctant to do so; he was then

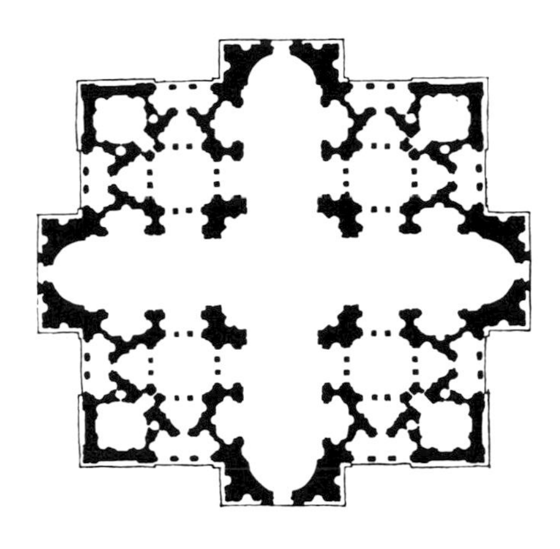

Bramante, 1506

Bramante-Raphael, 1515–20

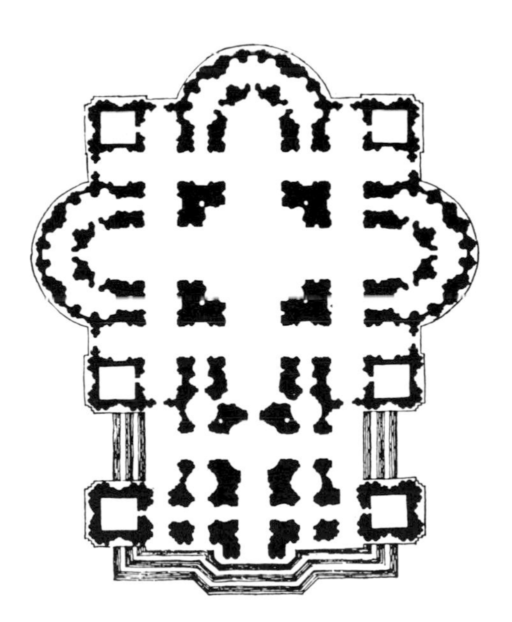

Sangallo, 1539

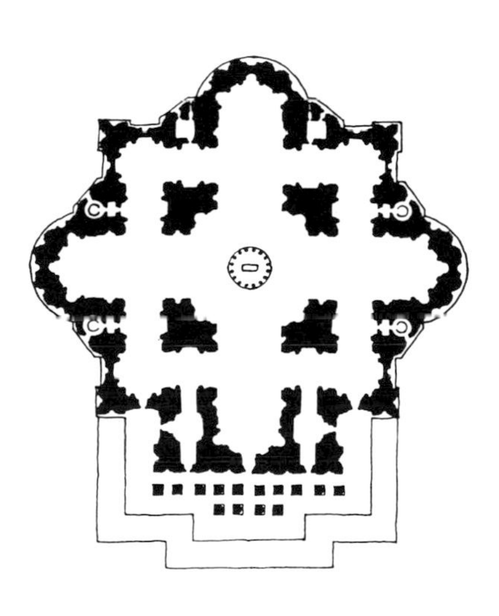

Michelangelo, 1546–64

142 Plans for St Peter's

seventy-one. But Paul III was insistent. Michelangelo finally agreed, insisting that he would work without payment and for his spiritual good. He was officially appointed on 1 January 1547, but he had already indicated his refusal to accept Sangallo's model and had produced a clay one of his own, followed by a wooden one, neither of which has survived.

In a letter, addressed early in 1547 to Bartolommeo Ferrantini, a Canon of St Peter's and Prefect of the Deputies of the Fabric, Michelangelo wrote the famous justification of Bramante as being

... as worthy an architect as any since ancient times. It was he who laid down the first plan of St Peter's, not full of confusion, but clear, pure, and full of light, so that it did not in any way damage the palace ... whoever departs from this order of Bramante's, as Sangallo has done, departs from the truth. And that this is so can be seen by anyone who looks with unprejudiced eyes at his model.

143 MAERTEN VAN HEEMSKERCK View of Old and New St Peter's 1532/35

144 MAERTEN VAN HEEMSKERCK View of central crossing of St Peter's 1532/35

He goes on to make the famous denunciation, that Sangallo's ambulatories would afford 'so many dark hiding places . . . that they would provide ample opportunity for innumerable villainies, such as the hiding of outlaws, the coining of false money, the raping of nuns and other crimes, so that at night when the church closes it would require twenty-five men to search out those who remained hidden . . .' His eulogy of Bramante was a noble reappraisal of someone whom he had, early in his Roman career, freely detested, just as his attack on Sangallo, which followed his sharp rejoinder that the model provided 'pasturage for sheep and oxen who know nothing of art', led to the bitter attacks on him by what he called 'the Sangallo sect'.

These attacks were made more intense by his demolition of parts of the basilica which Sangallo had built in accordance with his model. Not only did Michelangelo criticize the model for being over supplied with columns – the amount of fussy detail betrays Sangallo's inability to grasp the fundamentals of building on such a scale – but he insisted that retention of the outer walls of the hemicycles would impinge upon, and require the demolition of, parts of the palace, besides depriving the interior of light and involving huge and unnecessary expense. He therefore demolished these outer apsidal parts and made their corresponding inner hemicycles into the outer walls of the

145 ANTONIO DA SANGALLO Wooden model of St Peter's 1539–46

church. Later, he threw out the projected narthex so as to restore a proper central plan, and he eliminated the corner towers and reduced the size of the subsidiary chapels at the angles. The sniping continued with such severity that eventually Paul III issued a *motu proprio* on 5 October 1549 which gave Michelangelo absolute powers to do as he decided best. Paul died less than a month afterwards, but successive popes – Julius III, Paul IV and Pius IV – defended him against the further attacks of his relentless detractors (only Marcellus II, who died within weeks of his election, lent an ear to his enemies), and Pius IV laid it down categorically that Michelangelo's design was to be adhered to without alteration 'in perpetuity' – a vain hope.

148 What can now be seen is only partly Michelangelo's work, but what he achieved set the style for all later continuations and alterations. Building began with the southern hemicycle, which is organized in a clear system of a Giant Order of Corinthian pilasters set against a layering running like a pier from top to bottom, so that the surface is held together by the system of uprights and the massive entablature running across and uniting the major forms. Above the narrow cornice is an attic storey, divided by pilaster strips matching the system below. Though the authenticity of the design of this attic as Michelangelo's original work has been impugned, one of the few

146 MICHELANGELO Wooden model of the dome of St Peter's

little drawings (the tiny handful of drawings for St Peter's are all related to the dome) in a shaky hand is clearly for the attic system, and shows the pilaster strip divisions and both the niche with candelabrum and papal arms, and the vague outline of the larger rectangular window with the framing round it. No start was made on the construction of the dome until the late 1550s, but there is no reason to believe that the problem was not in the forefront of his mind throughout, and that he did not begin to plan the dome and drum long before. The presence of a project for the attic scribbled on an assistant's drawing for one of his ideas for the dome is hardly surprising.

The variety in size, shape and detailing of the windows and tabernacles between the huge pilasters of the outer walls and in the attic show the extraordinary versatility and richness of his imagination. The problem of the dome was finally resolved by della Porta and the engineer Domenico Fontana, who reared the pointed shell of the dome on the drum which Michelangelo had started but not completely finished. While it is certain that

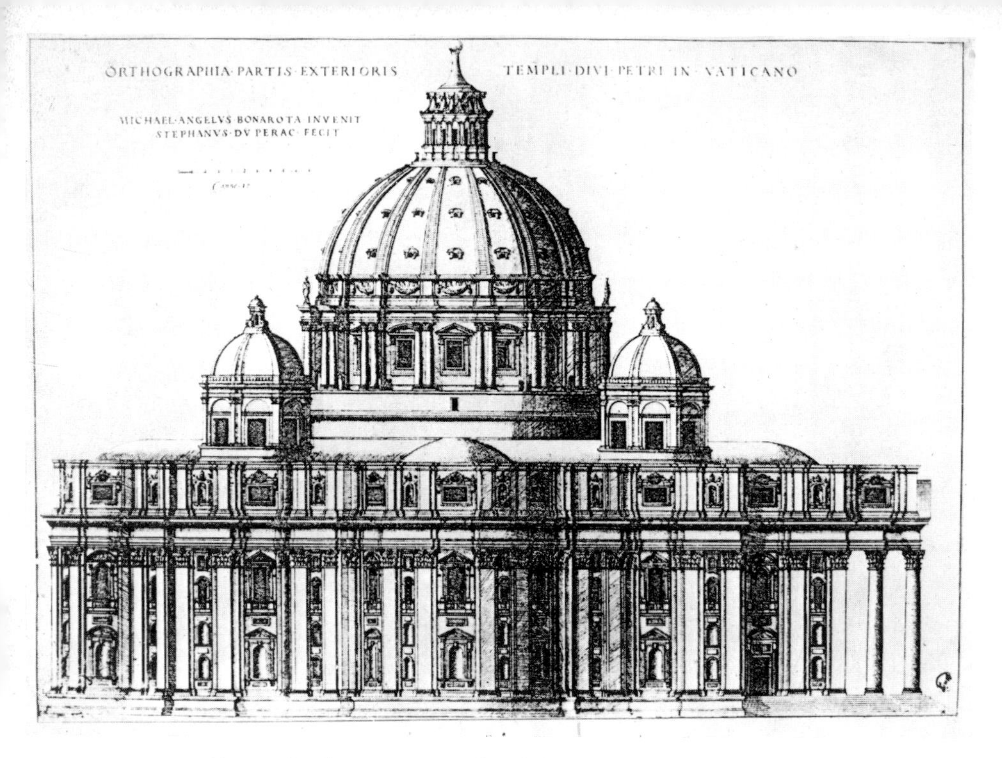

147 ETIENNE DUPÉRAC Engraving of Michelangelo's project for St Peter's 1568

Michelangelo originally planned a hemispherical dome, according to Bramante's first project of raising the dome of the Pantheon on the 'Temple of Peace' (the Basilica of Constantine), it is equally clear that the possibility of having to build the dome with a more pointed silhouette for reasons of stability had occurred to him, since two of the meagre four drawings which indicate what he had in mind in fact have a pointed shape. The large model of *146* the dome has a hemispherical interior profile, and a pointed exterior one, but this model may have been altered by della Porta.

Michelangelo left no indication of what he intended for the façade. It had to include the benediction loggia from which papal elections were announced, and from which the pope gave the Christmas and Easter blessings 'Urbi et Orbi' and the Holy Year blessings to the crowds below. Bramante offered no solution to this problem; the monstrous cavern in Sangallo's narthex would have entirely dwarfed any human being. *147* According to Dupérac's engravings Michelangelo seems to have planned a portico upheld by huge columns, but this would have involved putting the

148 St Peter's, view from the Vatican gardens

benediction loggia well into the shadows. He left sketches for the lantern of the dome, and these were largely used by della Porta in his eventual construction. After Michelangelo's death, Pirro Ligorio was appointed to succeed him, but was summarily dismissed for changing Michelangelo's designs. He was succeeded by Vignola, who continued the work without making any vital changes. When Vignola died in 1573, Pius IV asked Cavalieri for advice, and as a result della Porta was appointed. He probably built the two small subsidiary domes (which do not communicate with the interior and light nothing), built the main dome between 1588 and 1590, and the lantern between 1590 and 1593. The decision by the Borghese Pope Paul V to change the plan to a long nave was taken in 1607, and the work was completed by Maderno with the addition of three further bays and the narthex between 1608 and 1615. The addition made nonsense of the majestic dome, which from the front now sinks behind the length of the nave.

Vasari states that in 1550–51 Michelangelo rebuilt Bramante's Belvedere staircase as a double-ramped staircase of the type which he had designed for the Senate on the Campidoglio. Michelangelo's staircase was the first step in the reconstruction of Bramante's single-storey garden house at the end of the courtyard into the large two-storeyed villa with the much enlarged exedra, which eventually sprouted the strange superstructure designed by Pirro Ligorio in 1562–65. When the long nave was added to St Peter's, the *Pigna* – the antique bronze pine cone which had stood in the atrium of Old St Peter's – was placed at the top of Michelangelo's staircase.

During the time that Michelangelo was working on St Peter's, he undertook several other architectural commissions. In 1559 the Florentine

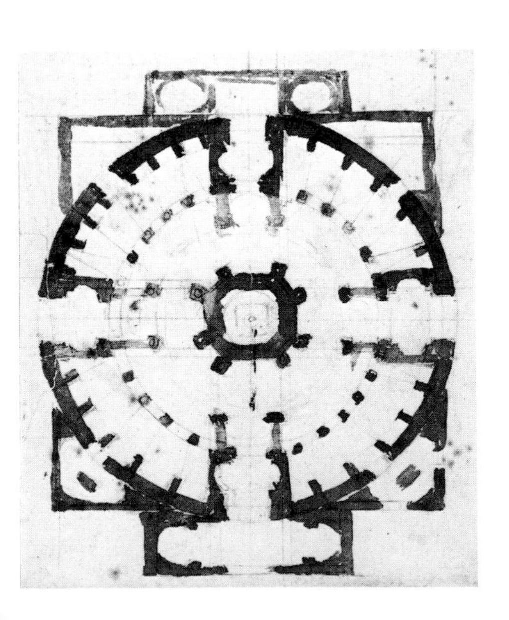

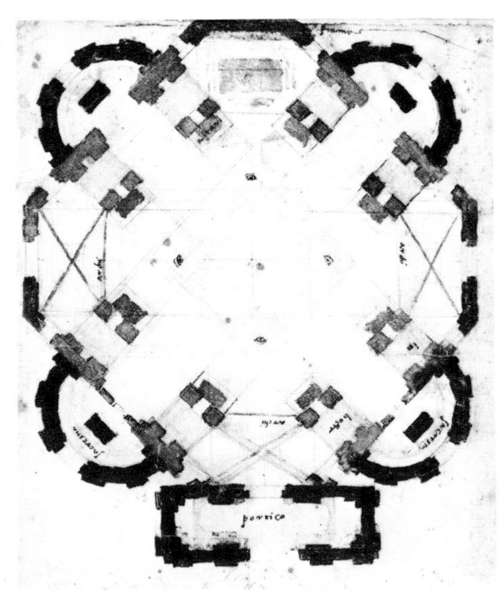

colony in Rome revived its long-delayed project of building a national church, and Michelangelo was asked for plans. Though he was now eighty-four years old, and oppressed by his cares at St Peter's, he prepared projects and his assistant Tiberio Calcagni made a model. Michelangelo returned to the original Sangallo idea of a centrally planned church, but his designs, of which three drawings survive, are far more complicated and spatially developed than the simple circle with radiating chapels that Sangallo had proposed. One of the difficulties with the project was that the site was on the river-bank and required massive foundations extending into the water. Michelangelo's projects all develop the theme of the central plan with several axes, two with a central altar, and all with domes. His concern with the problem of a central point, which the faithful are to circulate around but not cross, is clearly an extension of his experience of the spatial problems at St Peter's. Nothing, however, came of the proposals, and the present dull traditionally shaped church is a seventeenth-century construction.

149–151

Calcagni was also responsible, according to Vasari, for beginning the Cappella Sforza in Sta Maria Maggiore on Michelangelo's designs, but the deaths of the cardinal and the artist were followed by the death of Calcagni at the end of 1565. The remarkable plan of this chapel, with its off-centre central space covered by quadripartite vaulting springing from columns that project into the central space and at the same time define the elliptical side chapels and the square space of the main altar chapel, is matched by the use of travertine for its interior membering – a rare use internally of a building material normally only used for exteriors. The chapel has suffered much from the clumsy execution of assistants, so that its unusual plan, even more

152

153

149 MICHELANGELO (*far left*) Plan for S. Giovanni de' Fiorentini 1559

150 MICHELANGELO (*left*) Plan for S. Giovanni de' Fiorentini 1559

151 MICHELANGELO (*right*) Plan for S. Giovanni de' Fiorentini 1559

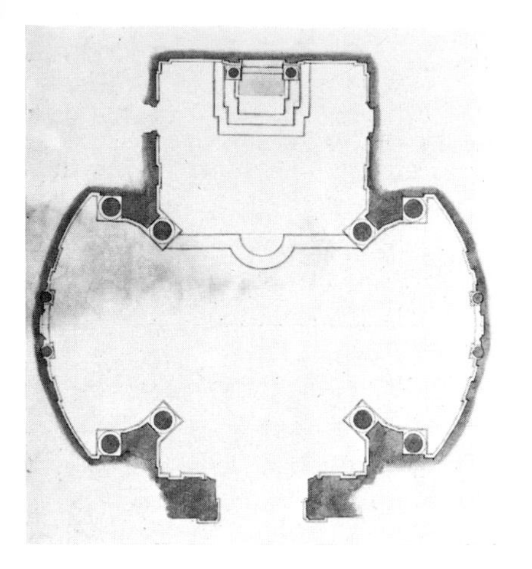

152 Plan of the Sforza Chapel, Sta Maria Maggiore *c.* 1560

153 Sforza Chapel, interior view

154 Porta Pia, façade (engraving) 1568

adventurous than the designs for S. Giovanni de' Fiorentini, remains its most striking feature. In all these designs, as at St Peter's, Michelangelo looks away from Renaissance stability and balance, and forward towards Baroque movement and dynamism, which is probably why they do not seem to have been acceptable to his contemporaries. Their future lay with Bernini and Borromini.

The Porta Pia resulted from Pius IV's decision in 1561 to build a new highway from the Quirinal to S. Agnese fuori le Mura – the Via Pia, now split up between the Via del Quirinale, the Via XX Settembre and the old Via Nomentana, which was straightened. For this he required a new city gate, for which Michelangelo provided a design. The gateway breaks with tradition in two ways: firstly, it faces inwards, whereas from antiquity onwards city gates presented their more ornate façades to the world outside, as a sign of the 'civilization' to be found within; secondly, it was an exercise in pure scenography, since the quarter through which the new road was built was almost uninhabited at the time. The design of the heavy portal is supported by drawings in Michelangelo's hand, and its eventual form is a conflation of several of these. There are also drawings associated with, but not actually for, the side windows on volutes (recalling his invention over forty years earlier of this type for the Medici palace in Florence) and for the small rectangular blind windows above them. The attic storey has little to do with Michelangelo. One was built, probably after his death, but it collapsed before 1587, and the present one is of 1853, based on the Faleti engraving.

154

The project for the Via Pia encouraged Pius IV to support the scheme for converting the central hall of the near-by Baths of Diocletian, which had survived in remarkably good state, into a church dedicated to Sta Maria degli Angeli. The rest of the structure was given to the Carthusians, who founded a monastery there. Michelangelo prepared designs for the church, but little now survives on the site since it was completely reconstructed in the eighteenth century, even its orientation being changed.

What are the characteristics of Michelangelo's architecture, other than its sheer beauty? Firstly, plasticity: it is the architecture of a sculptor who feels for volume and mass in his buildings as he felt for it in his sculpture, who envisages space as a moving, changing entity like the profiles presented by a figure as one changes one's viewpoint, who considers the structures which delimit space as masses which he moulds and shapes. Just as Michelangelo declared in one of his poems that the block of marble already contained the figure which, by his carving, he released from it, so in his architecture the converse applied: the function of the defining structures is to make tangible the space which already exists in the artist's vision.

Secondly, variety: the search for expressive form is pursued unremittingly. The various standard elements of plan, Orders, doors, windows, and so on, are subjected to an imaginative process which liberates Michelangelo from the strait-jacket of classical precedent, while he creates new forms which in turn inspire others. Vasari recognized the dangers which this presented, in that the liberties which Michelangelo took with classical canons were seized upon by lesser men as excuses for their artistic licence. But he also realized that Michelangelo's inventiveness enlarged the architectural vocabulary and provided new solutions for old problems.

Thirdly, scale: where his predecessors during the Renaissance had, with the exception of Bramante (as Michelangelo himself recognized), used antiquity as a quarry from which individual forms could be extracted and then adapted to whatever purpose they were required to serve, for Michelangelo the great lesson of antiquity was that of scale. 'Roma quanta fuit ipsa ruina docet' – what Rome was her very ruins teach us. The sheer size of the ruins of ancient Rome inspired him to create, not accretions of detail, piling up tiers of Orders and arcades on colonnades, as even so able a man as Sangallo did in his St Peter's model, but buildings which by their mass, their adjustment of the size of the parts to the size of the whole, have a scale which is commensurate with the total concept of the building.

CHAPTER SIX

The Sonnets. The Last Drawings and Sculptures

Michelangelo's poems are difficult, since his language is often very elliptical. Seventy-seven of his sonnets are known, as well as many madrigals, one of which was put to music by Jacob van Arcadelt, choirmaster of the Sistine Chapel choir. Some of the sonnets are on purely conventional themes, such as Dante, or returns of thanks in flowery phrases for gifts, or praises of the beauty of a friend's mistress. Most, however, have a much deeper personal significance, such as those either addressed to Tommaso Cavalieri, or which can be referred to him. The ambivalent character of these sonnets so troubled Michelangelo's great-nephew that when he published them in 1623 he deliberately changed – bowdlerized – some of them so as to disguise their true meaning. But the extravagant language which is apparent in Michelangelo's letters to Cavalieri also reappears in these sonnets, so that, in a sense, while their feeling is very genuine, the language is conventionalized. Michelangelo laments in sonnet XLVI* that he is an old man, and that his love has a quality of resignation with it, or that he 'sins not in loving natural things, if balance, measure, bounds, are kept' (XLV). Yet his sonnets to that paragon of virtue and serene religious exaltation, Vittoria Colonna, breathe the same kind of warm emotion and sensibility, and exactly the same passionate feeling is to be found in the purely religious sonnets, where the 'Signor mio caro' (LXXIII) is not human but Divine.

Among the most interesting sonnets is the early one (V) in which with bitter humour he describes the torments he endured while painting the Sistine Ceiling – his body bent like a bow, his skin stretched in front and shrunk behind, his brains driven back into his spine, his face bespattered with gobbets of paint until it looked like a mosaic pavement – ending with his everlasting cry that he was not a painter. There is also the fascinating sonnet (XV) in which he sets out the engaging thesis that 'the greatest artist has no thought that in the marble itself is not enclosed, and he alone arrives at it whose hand obeys his intellect', although the rest of the poem translates this magnificent idea into a more commonplace one: that his own good and ill condition is enclosed within the woman – clearly Vittoria Colonna – whom he addresses, and that from her supreme virtues he is unable, though his own fault, to recover anything but death.

* Sonnet numbers refer to the editions of Jennings and Symonds (see Bibliography).

155 MICHELANGELO *Crucifixion with the Virgin and St John c.* 1550/55

Finally, in the deepening faith of his old age, he sent Vasari in 1554 a sonnet (LXV) that begins 'Now that my life has run its course, and through stormy seas in a fragile boat I have arrived at the common harbour where all must give account for every action good or ill', and which ends with the poignant lines: 'The loving thoughts, vain and happy, which once I had – now I approach a double death; one is certain, the other threatens me. Painting and sculpture are no more able to comfort the soul which turns to the Divine love that to welcome us opens His arms upon the Cross.'

At the end of his life Michelangelo made a number of drawings, nearly all of religious subjects. Many of them develop themes which first appear in his work at the time of his friendship with Vittoria Colonna, developing after her untimely death a greater poignance, a deeper religious feeling, while technically they become less finished, more the expression of ideas which flow from his profound pessimism, his deepening faith, his loneliness, and the appalling frustrations he suffered at the hands of uncomprehending

156 MICHELANGELO *Crucifixion c.* 1560

officials. That he was continually supported by a succession of intelligent popes did not always counterbalance the slights and indignities he endured at the hands of small men with small minds, intent upon selfish and mercenary ends. In these drawings he found a refuge, just as he did in continuing, despite age and infirmity, to attempt the creation of his last sculptures. The sequence of *Crucifixion* drawings probably stems from his idea of a memorial to *155, 156* Vittoria Colonna, and therefore had, so to speak, a fixed creative impulse; the *Annunciation* drawings date probably from 1560 or thereabouts; the huge *158* cartoon of the *Holy Family with Saints* is somewhat earlier – probably about *157* 1553, since it is not mentioned by Condivi who made a very bad small painting based on it. What the cartoon was made for is unknown, neither has the subject been properly elucidated. That the old man on the Virgin's right, whom she apparently repels, is Joseph is more than likely; the identity of the young saint to whom she turns and the meaning of his gesture have so far defied explanation. The forms have the massive quality developed when he was working on the Cappella Paolina frescoes, and none of the hesitancy, the

157 MICHELANGELO *Holy Family with Saints c.* 1553

158 MICHELANGELO *Annunciation* c. 1560

fumbling for form, which appear in his later *Crucifixion* drawings and in the superb very late *Virgin and Child*, which are all searches for form, struggles for expression. These late drawings are, in a sense, the counterpart of his late religious poems – faith made visible, tangible.

During the long years when Michelangelo's main concern was with architecture, and particularly with the building of St Peter's, he worked on two groups of the *Pietà*, neither of which was finished and both of which he mutilated. One, now in Florence Cathedral, is recorded by Vasari in his 1550 edition (which was in great part written three years earlier), and by Condivi, so that the time-span for this group is about fifteen years. At the back of the group of four figures is Nicodemus (sometimes identified as Joseph of Arimathea), who traditionally carried Christ's body to the tomb. Michelangelo has given his own features to this figure, who holds Christ's right arm with one hand and steadies the Virgin with the other. She holds her Son on one of her knees, His head drooping against hers, but Christ's left arm has been badly broken and ill repaired, and His left leg is missing. Apparently, this leg once crossed the Virgin's knee to reach the ground on the far side of her figure. According to Vasari, the block contained flaws of emery which struck sparks from the chisel, and enraged by these defects and also by the nagging of his servant and companion Urbino, who died in 1555, Michelangelo broke up the group. Later he gave it to a friend, who got Tiberio Calcagni to repair it; according to Vasari, Calcagni added 'God knows how many new pieces', and attempts to mend the statue are obvious from Christ's left arm, and from the square hole which has been drilled at the place where the leg was broken off, patently for the keying-in of another piece of marble. Calcagni worked on the Magdalen, reducing her to an oddly diminutive figure of utter conventionality, but further reworking was prevented by his death in 1565. The group, which Michelangelo originally destined for his own tomb, was not taken to Florence until about 1674, but the Grand Duke Cosimo III did not consider it worthy to be placed in the Medici Chapel. After being in the crypt of S. Lorenzo it was removed in 1721 to the cathedral. The 1566 inventory of the goods of Daniele da Volterra mentions 'a knee in marble from the *Pietà* by Michelangelo' – probably the left leg which Michelangelo broke off. What does survive from the group is the pathos, the sense of helpless tragedy, the poignant grief.

159

The *Rondanini Pietà*, so called from the palace where for many years it stood in the courtyard, presents quite different problems. A drawing records five states in Michelangelo's thinking for a Deposition group: two of them with the dead Christ borne between two figures, one on either side; three with the dead Christ supported by a single figure standing behind Him. In all three of these two-figure sketches the body of Christ sags forward, the head

161 *160*

159 Michelangelo *Pietà c.* 1547–55

160 MICHELANGELO Sketches for the *Rondanini Pietà* c. 1555

hanging over, the right arm dangling forward while the left arm is suspended over the restraining hand of the supporting figure. The first state of the *Rondanini Pietà* must represent the translation into marble of this two-figure group, and the figure behind Christ must originally have been intended as a man, since it is inconceivable that the Virgin should ever have been represented with one stalwart leg bare to the knee. Moreover, the proportions of the Virgin, if this leg could be believed ever to have been hers, are totally wrong; the leg is too short for the body. According to Vasari, after Michelangelo had broken the *Pietà* with four figures 'it was necessary for him to find another marble, so that he could pass some time every day in carving; he got another piece of marble in which another Pietà had been roughed out, different and much smaller'. What went wrong with this first group, in which both of Christ's legs and one of His arms are in a partially finished state, is unknown; now, Christ's body melts into the body of the Virgin so that both can barely be deciphered as separate forms through their mutilation and the fumbling struggles of a very old man to force his trembling hand to follow the vision in his mind's eye. They express with extreme pathos the frailty of age, the helplessness of an old man facing death, and his fervent belief in the redeeming power of the sacrifice he was still seeking to portray. Daniele da Volterra recorded that he was working on this group six days before his death, and death came for him on the evening of 18 February 1564, in his eighty-ninth year.

161 MICHELANGELO *Rondanini Pietà* 1555–64

PIETA DI MICHEL ANGELO BVONAROTA

CHAPTER SEVEN

Aftermath

It was quite obvious to his contemporaries that, in the light of Michelangelo's works, all the arts – whether painting, sculpture or architecture – had changed decisively.

The careers of Leonardo da Vinci, Raphael and Michelangelo totally changed the concept of the artist as a craftsman employed to execute a commission. This change evolved from Leonardo's attitude towards the 'noble' qualities of art and, by extension, of its practitioner – ideas which Leonardo confined to painting, and from which he specifically excluded sculpture as being a messy manual labour – and also from the social position attained by Raphael and Michelangelo. This rise in the social scale was partly a result of the patronage of Julius II – a great pope, requiring great works, and demanding the almost exclusive right to the services of the best artists he could find. It also stemmed from Julius's recognition of the nature of genius, and it was followed almost as a policy by succeeding popes. The papacy, as the agent of the Church in commissioning important works, could also command performance by the artists of its choice.

The very quality of the performance of these artists inevitably had a powerful effect on what came after them, chiefly because they had no successors. None of the three had a pupil who even began to approach his master. Only Giulio Romano achieved an independent status, and that mainly because Raphael died so young and because Giulio created for himself a separate career in Mantua. With them, genius was a personal and untransmissible attribute. The sentimental simperings of Luini's imitations of Leonardo's famous smile and *chiaroscuro*, the vapid attempts of Penni to copy Raphael's Madonnas, the fumbling inadequacies of Michelangelo's various followers, from Venusti's timid copies of his Crucifixion drawings, Condivi's incompetent rendering of the *Holy Family* cartoon, Montelupo's characterless figures on the Julius Tomb, Urbano's botching of the *Christ of the Minerva*, Calcagni's feeble reworking of the Magdalen in the Florence *Pietà* . . . the list is long and sad. That Michelangelo's great architectural works fared better was largely because the style he created had to be adhered to, given the amount of St Peter's he had built before he died. Nevertheless the design of the basilica was radically changed, and the profile of the dome altered (to give them their due, della Porta and Fontana did not do this through a wanton desire for change, although at the Conservatori della Porta distinguished himself by his unfortunate 'improvements').

It has been argued that Michelangelo left works unfinished because he had said what he wanted to say when that stage of the work was reached, so that further finishing was unnecessary. This cannot be a serious argument. It is true that Condivi said that the state of incompleteness 'need not impair the finished beauty of the work', and that Vasari describes how Michelangelo's inability to be satisfied caused him to stop when he was aware of the slightest divagation from his ideal. In discussing the *Madonna and Child* in the Medici Chapel Vasari remarks that it is possible to see in the imperfect block the perfection of the completed work. Neoplatonic philosophy argued that the concept has priority over realization, since realization is tainted with the imperfections that result from achievement falling below the concept, and it also advanced the ideas of spirituality in art being more compatible with the realization of the inner concept than with the actual realization of a subject. For more than a century Renaissance art had concentrated on the re-creation of natural appearances so that the adumbration of an idea, and the non-finish of a form, had to be identified with the unattained re-creation of nature, while leaving it open why the artist had not completed his work. One point of major importance is that while plenty of reasons have been found for Michelangelo's unfinished work, they apply to sculpture rather than to painting, and to Michelangelo rather than to anyone else. They have the strong look of an argument made to fit unalterable circumstances, rather than one which the artist himself would have advanced. His patrons vied with one another for works by his hand; this in itself was a novel state of affairs, and one which also applied to Raphael. But if, as in the case of the *Pitti Tondo* or the *Taddei Tondo*, there was no other way of attaining to the glory of possession, then the state of incompleteness was one for which excellent arguments could be – and were – found.

Michelangelo's immensely long life, and the fame which he attained, gave his work an almost total and, except for the attacks on the *Last Judgment*, uncritical acceptance, and the objectors to the nudes in the *Last Judgment* were very rarely artists, but theologians, prelates . . . and Aretino. For the rest of the artistic confraternity, the type of nude he created, and his almost exclusive concentration on the male nude, drove them to compete on ground which none – until Bernini – had either the imagination or the ability to follow. The convolutions of pose, the exaggerations of musculature, the piling up of nudes often in incongruous conglomeration, show how much his imitators failed to understand his art and distorted his style. Particularly was this true of northerners attracted to the imitation of

Italian art as signs of their advanced knowledge, superior ability, and up-to-dateness, but in general they were, like Spranger, unable to do more than parody the art they tried to emulate.

In sculpture, Michelangelo's *non-finito* had little effect; few artists dared to flout the customs imposed by long practice, risk the refusal of their works by indignant commissioners, or claim the kind of immunity from convention which was automatically granted to him by leaving works in an obviously unfinished state. Rodin did it, but not as Michelangelo did; Rodin did it for effect, deliberately using the rough unfinished parts of his block to contrast with highly finished surfaces juxtaposed to them. There were few sculptors of note in the same generation as Michelangelo: Sansovino worked mainly in Venice and largely as an architect; in Florence only Danti, Ammanati and Cellini were artists of any real significance. In the next generation came Giovanni da Bologna in Florence, supreme creator of the elegant, twisted pose inspired by Michelangelo and expressed in beautiful highly worked surfaces, and Vittoria in Venice, creator of fine decorative sculpture and splendid portrait busts.

In architecture, it could be argued that, as Vasari had predicted, Michelangelo's influence was baleful in that the liberties he took with classical forms encouraged lesser men to copy his ideas. But, in fact, the next generation of architects in Rome were dominated by Vignola, whose 'back-to-Bramante' type of classicism left little room for Michelangelesque extravagances; and outside Rome, Palladio became the supreme exponent of classical forms, and where he looks at Michelangelo he does so with intelligent understanding in which imitation has no place. The architects of the next generation were inspired by quite different ideas and aims, even when they were constrained, as Maderno was at St Peter's, to follow the models Michelangelo had set. It was not until Borromini that the influence of Michelangelo's forms really began to work through, and then in so changed a context that imitation is no longer an applicable term.

In what way, then, can Michelangelo be said to have changed everything? Firstly, by the force of personality. After Michelangelo, genius was more readily recognized, appreciated, sought after. Once he had been recognized as an exceptional talent, the artist was allowed more say in the design and execution of his work, was less circumscribed by the limitations of contemporary taste, was freer to experiment and to innovate. The careers of Palladio, Bernini, Rubens, Wren and Mansart are, in a way, a natural follow-on to Michelangelo's. Secondly, by the creation of a new vocabulary of form, though not one which his followers could always assimilate, and by the dovetailing of supreme technical achievement to the grandest imaginative power. Thirdly, by his universality. He was equally creative, imaginative and competent in all the three arts. Fourthly, in a negative sense. After him there were no fresh fields to conquer, no pastures new to explore, until in a later generation artists abandoned the notion of competition and emulation, and turned to the expression of quite different aims, as was the case with the Carracci and Caravaggio. Bernini, in his greatest tombs, nodded in the direction of the Medici Chapel; in his architecture, he acknowledged the mastery of his predecessor at St Peter's by creating on the same scale; at S. Andrea al Quirinale, he revealed the influence of the designs for S. Giovanni de' Fiorentini; at the Chigi palace and in the Louvre projects, he remembered the grandeur and simplicity of the Farnese and Conservatori palaces: but these were inspirations and standards to be equalled, not forms to be imitated. Lastly, by his example. Michelangelo became as no other before or since the archetype of the artist: dedicated, solitary, single-minded, tormented, harassed, unsatisfied, and undefeated.

Bibliography

The great Michelangelo bibliography by Ernst Steinmann and Rudolf Wittkower, Leipzig, 1927, lists everything from 1510 to 1926 and amounts to 2,107 items. It was continued to 1930 by H.W. Schmidt, to 1942 by P. Cherubelli, and to 1962 by Paola Barocchi in her edition of Vasari's Life of Michelangelo. The list was brought up to 1964 by Peter Meller in the commemorative volume for the fourth centenary of Michelangelo's death. *R.I.L.A.* (*International Repertory of the Literature of Art*), published twice a year, started in 1975 and lists all recent books and articles. It should be found in all major libraries.

The following books, arranged alphabetically, will be of help to the student. All of them contain extensive bibliographies. No periodical literature appears here, for reasons of space.

ACKERMAN, JAMES S., *The Architecture of Michelangelo*, 2 vols, London and New York, 1966 (revised edition); paperback edition, with abridged catalogue by John Newman, Harmondsworth, 1970

EINEM, HERBERT VON, *Michelangelo*, London, 1973; paperback edition, London, 1976 and New York, 1977

ETTLINGER, L.D., *The Complete Paintings of Michelangelo*, Classics of World Art, London and New York, 1969 (the English version of the Rizzoli series, of which the corresponding volume on Michelangelo's sculpture by Umberto Baldini, Milan, 1973, has not appeared in English)

HARTT, FREDERICK, *Michelangelo* (paintings), New York and London, 1965

——, *Michelangelo: the Complete Sculpture*, New York, 1968 and London, 1969

——, *The Drawings of Michelangelo*, New York, 1970 and London 1971

HIBBARD, HOWARD, *Michelangelo*, New York and London, 1975; paperback edition, New York, 1976 and Harmondsworth, 1978

SALVINI, ROBERTO, *The Hidden Michelangelo*, Oxford and New York, 1978

STEINBERG, LEO, *Michelangelo's Last Paintings*, London and New York, 1975

WILDE, JOHANNES, *Italian Drawings in the British Museum: Michelangelo and his Studio*, London, 1953

——, *Michelangelo: Six Lectures*, Oxford, 1979

Vasari and Condivi

BULL, GEORGE (trans.), *Giorgio Vasari. Life of Michelangelo Buonarroti*, London, 1971

——, *Giorgio Vasari. The Lives of the Artists*, Harmondsworth and Baltimore, 1965

WOHL, ALICE SEDGWICK, and HELMUT WOHL (trans.), *Ascanio Condivi's Life of Michelangelo*, Baton Rouge and Oxford, 1976

Letters and Poems

RAMSDEN, E.H. (trans.), *The Letters of Michelangelo*, 2 vols, London and Stanford, 1963 (English text only)

GILBERT, CREIGHTON, and ROBERT N. LINSCOTT (trans.), *Complete Poems and Selected Letters of Michelangelo*, New York, 1965 (English text only)

JENNINGS, ELIZABETH (trans.), *The Sonnets of Michelangelo*, London, 1961 (English text only)

SYMONDS, J.A. (trans.), *The Sonnets of Michelangelo*, London, 1950 (first published in 1878: Italian and English texts)

Background History

HALE, J.R., *Florence and the Medici: the Pattern of Control*, London, 1977

PASTOR, LUDWIG VON, *The History of the Popes*, vols V–XVI (many editions and various publishers)

RUBINSTEIN, NICOLAI, *The Government of Florence under the Medici*, Oxford, 1966

List of Illustrations

Measurements are given in inches followed by centimetres, height preceding width, unless otherwise indicated

part of Michelangelo's *Battle of Cascina*, *c.* 1542, cartoon. Grisaille on panel. By kind permission of Viscount Coke, Holkham Hall, Norfolk

43 Michelangelo. Drawing for the *Battle of Cascina*, *c.* 1504. Black chalk over stylus preparations, heightened with white, $7\frac{5}{8} \times 10\frac{1}{2}$ (19·5 × 26·5). Albertina, Vienna (S.R. 157 v)

44 Andrea Mantegna (*c.* 1431–1506). *Entombment*. Engraving, 13 × 18 (33 × 46). British Museum, London (B.3)

45 *Laocoön*, Hellenistic original of *c.* 150 BC or later Roman copy. Rediscovered, Rome, 1506. Marble, h. 96 (244). Vatican Museums

46 Michelangelo. *Entombment*, *c.* 1506. Panel, $63\frac{2}{3} \times 59$ (161 × 149). National Gallery, London

47 Sistine Chapel, view of interior. Vatican

48 Michelangelo. Sketch for decoration of the Sistine Ceiling, with studies of arms and hands, 1508–09. Pen over leadpoint, black chalk, $10\frac{3}{4} \times 15\frac{1}{4}$ (27·5 × 39). British Museum, London (W.7 r)

49 Michelangelo. Sistine Ceiling, 1508–12. Fresco, approx. 42 ft, 8 in × 132 ft (13 m × 40 m). Vatican

50 Michelangelo. *Ezekiel*. Fresco. Sistine Ceiling, Vatican

51 Michelangelo. *Joel*. Fresco. Sistine Ceiling, Vatican

52 Michelangelo. *Isaiah*. Fresco. Sistine Ceiling, Vatican

53 Michelangelo. *Daniel*. Fresco. Sistine Ceiling, Vatican

54 Michelangelo. *Jeremiah*. Fresco. Sistine Ceiling, Vatican

55 Michelangelo. *Zechariah*. Fresco. Sistine Ceiling, Vatican

56 Michelangelo. *Jonah*. Fresco. Sistine Ceiling, Vatican

57 Michelangelo. *Delphic Sibyl*. Fresco. Sistine Ceiling, Vatican

58 Michelangelo. *Erythraean Sibyl*. Fresco. Sistine Ceiling, Vatican

59 Michelangelo. *Persian Sibyl*. Fresco. Sistine Ceiling, Vatican

60 Michelangelo. *Libyan Sibyl*. Fresco. Sistine Ceiling, Vatican

61 Michelangelo. *Cumaean Sibyl*. Fresco. Sistine Ceiling, Vatican

62 Michelangelo. Sistine Ceiling, detail. Vatican

63 Michelangelo. *The Deluge*. Fresco. Sistine Ceiling, Vatican

64 Michelangelo. *The Sacrifice of Noah*. Fresco. Sistine Ceiling, Vatican

65 Michelangelo. *The Drunkenness of Noah*. Fresco. Sistine Ceiling, Vatican

66 Michelangelo. *The Fall and Expulsion*. Fresco. Sistine Ceiling, Vatican

67 Michelangelo. *The Creation of Eve*. Fresco. Sistine Ceiling, Vatican

68 Michelangelo. *The Creation of Adam*. Fresco. Sistine Ceiling, Vatican

69 Michelangelo. *God separating Earth from Water*. Fresco. Sistine Ceiling, Vatican

70 Michelangelo. *The Creation of the Sun, Moon and Stars*. Fresco. Sistine Ceiling, Vatican

71 Michelangelo. *God separating Light from Darkness*. Fresco. Sistine Ceiling, Vatican

72 Michelangelo. *David and Goliath*. Fresco. Sistine Ceiling, Vatican

73 Michelangelo. *Judith and Holofernes*. Fresco. Sistine Ceiling, Vatican

74 Michelangelo. *Esther and Haman*. Fresco. Sistine Ceiling, Vatican

75 Michelangelo. *The Brazen Serpent*. Fresco. Sistine Ceiling, Vatican

76 Michelangelo. *Ancestors of Christ: Abiud and Eliachim*. Fresco. Sistine Ceiling, Vatican

77 Michelangelo. First pair of *Ignudi* with part of *The Drunkenness of Noah*. Fresco. Sistine Ceiling, Vatican

78 Michelangelo. *Ancestors of Christ: Manasses and Amon*. Fresco. Sistine Ceiling, Vatican

79 Michelangelo. Study for the *Libyan Sibyl*, 1511. Red chalk, $11\frac{1}{4} \times 8\frac{3}{8}$ (28·5 × 20·5). Metropolitan Museum of Art, New York (24.197.2 r): Purchase, 1924, Joseph Pulitzer Bequest

80 Michelangelo. Study for a *putto* and for the right hand of the *Libyan Sibyl*, with sketches for the Julius Tomb, 1511 and 1513. Red chalk, pen, $11\frac{1}{4} \times 7\frac{5}{8}$ (28·5 × 19·5). Ashmolean Museum, Oxford (P.297 r)

81 Michelangelo. Tomb of Julius II. Marble. San Pietro in Vincoli, Rome

82 Drawing after Michelangelo's 1513 project for the tomb of Julius II. Pen and ink, $20\frac{5}{8} \times 13\frac{3}{8}$ (52·5 × 39). Staatliche Museen zu Berlin (East) (k.d.z.15.306)

83 Michelangelo. *Dying Slave*, 1513/16. Marble, h. $90\frac{1}{8}$ (229). Louvre, Paris

84 Michelangelo. *Rebellious Slave*, 1513/16. Marble, h. $84\frac{5}{8}$ (215). Louvre, Paris

85 Donatello (*c.* 1386–1466). *St John the Evangelist*, 1410–15. Marble, h. $82\frac{1}{2}$ (210). Museo dell' Opera del Duomo, Florence

86 Michelangelo. *Moses*, 1513/16. Marble, h. $92\frac{1}{2}$ (235). Tomb of Julius II, San Pietro in Vincoli, Rome

87 Michelangelo. *Risen Christ* (*Christ of the Minerva*), 1519/20. Marble, h. $80\frac{3}{4}$ (205). Santa Maria sopra Minerva, Rome

88 Giuliano da Sangallo (1445–1516). Drawing for the façade of San Lorenzo, Florence. Uffizi, Florence (Arch. 281)

89 Michelangelo. Sketch for the façade of San Lorenzo, Florence, 1517. Red and black chalks, $5\frac{1}{2} \times 7\frac{1}{8}$ (14 × 18). Casa Buonarroti, Florence (47A)

90 Wooden model for the façade of San Lorenzo, Florence, *c.* 1517, probably executed by Urbano to Michelangelo's final design. Casa Buonarroti, Florence

91a Section of the Old Sacristy, San Lorenzo, Florence. From W. and E. Paatz, *Die Kirchen von Florenz*, Frankfurt, 1940–53

91b Plan of the Old Sacristy, San Lorenzo, Florence. Drawing Linda Murray

92a Section of the New Sacristy (Medici Chapel), San Lorenzo, Florence. From C. von Stegmann and H. von Geymüller, *Die Architektur der Renaissance in Toskana*, Munich, 1885–1909

92b Michelangelo. Plan of the New Sacristy (Medici Chapel), San Lorenzo, Florence. Drawing Linda Murray

93 San Lorenzo, Florence. View of façade with Medici Chapel (right)

94 Michelangelo. Medici Chapel, 1520–34, San Lorenzo, Florence, view looking towards entrance wall

95 Michelangelo. Tomb of Giuliano de' Medici, Duke of Nemours (d. 1516), probably 1531–33. Marble, h. of figure of Giuliano 68 (173). Medici Chapel, San Lorenzo, Florence

96 Michelangelo. Tomb of Lorenzo de' Medici, Duke of Urbino (d. 1519), *c.* 1524. Marble, h. of figure of Lorenzo $70\frac{1}{8}$ (178·5). Medici Chapel, San Lorenzo, Florence

97 Michelangelo. *Day*. Marble (unfinished), $34\frac{1}{4} \times 72\frac{3}{4}$ (87 × 185). Tomb of Giuliano de' Medici, Medici Chapel, San Lorenzo, Florence

98 Michelangelo. *Night*. Marble, $24\frac{3}{4} \times 76\frac{3}{8}$ (63 × 194). Tomb of Giuliano de' Medici. Medici Chapel, San Lorenzo, Florence

99 Michelangelo. *Madonna and Child*. Marble, h. with base $99\frac{1}{2}$ (253). Medici Chapel, San Lorenzo, Florence

100 Michelangelo. Sketch for a double tomb, 1520/21. Pen, $8\frac{1}{4} \times 6\frac{3}{8}$ (21 × 15·5). British Museum, London (W.28 r)

101 Michelangelo. Medici Chapel, San Lorenzo, Florence, view of cupola

102 Michelangelo. Laurenziana Library, San Lorenzo, Florence, begun 1524. Section and plan after Apolloni, from James S. Ackerman, *The Architecture of Michelangelo*, vol. II, London, 1961

103 Michelangelo. Laurenziana Library, San Lorenzo, Florence, vestibule wall

104 Michelangelo. Laurenziana Library, San Lorenzo, Florence, vestibule staircase

105 Giovanni Battista Piranesi (1720–78). Tomb of Annia Regilla. Etching, detail, from the *Magnificenza . . . de' Romani*, 1761

106 Michelangelo. Laurenziana Library, San Lorenzo, Florence, reading-room

107 Michelangelo. *Bearded Slave*. Marble (unfinished), h. with base $100\frac{3}{4}$ (255·5). Accademia delle Belle Arti, Florence

108 Michelangelo. *Victory*, *c.* 1530/33. Marble, h. $102\frac{3}{4}$ (261). Palazzo Vecchio, Florence

109 Michelangelo. *Apollo* (*David*), *c.* 1530. Marble, h. with base $57\frac{1}{2}$ (146). Museo Nazionale (Bargello), Florence

110 Michelangelo. Drawing for a *Resurrection*, 1512. Black chalk, $14\frac{3}{8} \times 8\frac{3}{4}$ (36 × 22). Royal Library, Windsor (12768). Reproduced by gracious permission of Her Majesty Queen Elizabeth II

111 Michelangelo. Drawing for a *Resurrection*, *c.* 1525/30. Black chalk, $9\frac{1}{2} \times 13\frac{5}{8}$ (24 × 34·5). Royal Library, Windsor (12767 r). Reproduced by gracious permission of Her Majesty Queen Elizabeth II

112 Michelangelo. Drawing for a *Resurrection*, 1532/33. Black chalk, $12\frac{3}{4} \times 11\frac{1}{4}$ (32·5 × 28·5). British Museum, London (W.52)

113 Luca Signorelli (*c.* 1441/50–1523). *The Last Judgment: The Damned*, 1500–04. Fresco. Orvieto Cathedral

114 Michelangelo. *The Last Judgment*, 1534–41. Fresco, 45 ft × 40 ft (13·7 m × 12·2 m). Sistine Chapel, Vatican

115 Michelangelo. *The Last Judgment*, detail of the Resurrection of the Dead. Fresco. Sistine Chapel, Vatican

116 Michelangelo. *The Last Judgment*, detail of Christ in Judgment. Fresco. Sistine Chapel, Vatican

117 Michelangelo. *The Last Judgment*, detail of St Peter and St Bartholomew. Fresco. Sistine Chapel, Vatican

118 Michelangelo. *The Last Judgment*, detail of the Damned. Fresco. Sistine Chapel, Vatican

119 Michelangelo. *Divine Head*, 1532/34? Drawing, red chalk, $8 \times 6\frac{1}{2}$ (20·5 × 16·5). Ashmolean Museum, Oxford (P.315)

120 Michelangelo. *Divine Head*, 1532/34? Drawing, black chalk, $11\frac{1}{4} \times 9\frac{1}{4}$ (28·5 × 23·5). British Museum, London (W.42 r)

121 Michelangelo. *The Punishment of Tityus*, 1532. Drawing, black chalk, $7\frac{1}{2} \times 13$ (19 × 33). Royal Library, Windsor (12771 r). Reproduced by gracious permission of Her Majesty Queen Elizabeth II

122 Michelangelo. *The Fall of Phaethon*, 1533. Drawing, black chalk, $16\frac{1}{4} \times 9\frac{1}{4}$ (41·3 × 23·5). Royal Library, Windsor (12766 r). Reproduced by gracious permission of Her Majesty Queen Elizabeth II

123 Michelangelo. *Children's Bacchanal*, 1533? Drawing, red chalk, $10\frac{3}{4} \times 15\frac{1}{4}$ (27·5 × 39). Royal Library, Windsor (12777). Reproduced by gracious permission of Her Majesty Queen Elizabeth II

124 Michelangelo. *Archers shooting at a Herm*, 1533? Drawing, red chalk, $8\frac{1}{2} \times 12\frac{5}{8}$ (21·5 × 32). Royal Library, Windsor (12778). Reproduced by gracious permission of Her Majesty Queen Elizabeth II

125 Michelangelo. *The Dream of Human Life*, 1533/34? Drawing, black chalk, stippled, $15\frac{5}{8} \times 11$ (39·5 × 28). Courtesy the Executors of the Estate of Count Antoine Seilern

126 Michelangelo. *Crucifixion*, *c.* 1540. Drawing, black chalk, $14\frac{5}{8} \times 10\frac{5}{8}$ (37 × 27). British Museum, London (W.67)

127 Michelangelo. *Pietà*, 1538/40. Drawing, black chalk, $11\frac{5}{8} \times 7\frac{5}{8}$ (29·5 × 19·5). Isabella Stewart Gardner Museum, Boston

128 Michelangelo. *Holy Family* (*Madonna of Silence*), 1540? Drawing, red chalk, $15 \times 11\frac{1}{4}$ (38 × 28·5). Private Collection

129 Michelangelo. *Brutus*, *c.* 1540. Marble, h. without base $29\frac{1}{8}$ (74). Museo Nazionale (Bargello), Florence

130 Michelangelo. *Rachel* (*Contemplative Life*). Marble, h. $77\frac{1}{2}$ (197). Tomb of Julius II, San Pietro in Vincoli, Rome

131 Michelangelo. *Leah* (*Active Life*). Marble, h. $82\frac{1}{2}$ (209). Tomb of Julius II, San Pietro in Vincoli, Rome

132 Michelangelo. *The Conversion of St Paul*, 1542–45. Fresco, 20 ft, 6 in × 21 ft, 9 in (6·25 m × 6·61 m). Cappella Paolina, Vatican

133 Michelangelo. *The Crucifixion of St Peter*, 1546–50. Fresco, 20 ft, 6 in × 21 ft, 9 in (6·25 m × 6·61 m). Cappella Paolina, Vatican

134 Michelangelo. Drawing for the fortifications of Florence, 1528/29. Pen, wash, traces of red chalk, $16\frac{1}{4} \times 22\frac{3}{8}$ (41 × 57). Casa Buonarroti, Florence (13 A r)

135 Italian School. Drawing of the Capitoline Hill, Rome, *c.* 1554–60. Cabinet des Dessins, Louvre, Paris (11028)

136 Etienne Dupérac (1525–1604). Engraving of Michelangelo's design for the Capitoline Hill, Rome, 1568

137 Michelangelo. Piazza del Campidoglio, Rome

138 Michelangelo and Giacomo della Porta (1540–1602). Conservatori Palace, Rome, designed before 1546

139 Antonio da Sangallo (1483–1546) and Michelangelo. Farnese Palace, Rome, entrance façade

140 Michelangelo. Farnese Palace, Rome, top-storey window on courtyard

141 Michelangelo and Giacomo Vignola (1507–73). Farnese Palace, Rome, courtyard

142 Plans for St Peter's, Rome. (1) Bramante, 1506; (2) Bramante-Raphael, 1515–20; (3) Antonio da Sangallo, 1539; (4) Michelangelo, 1546–64. From James S. Ackerman, *The Architecture of Michelangelo*, vol II, London, 1961

143 Maerten van Heemskerck (1498–1574). View of Old and New St Peter's, 1532/35. Pen and ink and wash. Kupferstichkabinett, Staatliche Museen, West Berlin

144 Maerten van Heemskerck (1498–1574). View of central crossing of St Peter's while under construction, 1532/35. Kupferstichkabinett, Staatliche Museen, West Berlin

145 Antonio da Sangallo (1483–1546). Wooden model of St Peter's, 1539–46. Museo di San Pietro, Rome

146 Michelangelo. Wooden model of the dome of St Peter's. Museo di San Pietro, Rome

147 Etienne Dupérac (1525–1604). Engraving of Michelangelo's project for St Peter's, Rome, 1568

148 St Peter's, Rome. View from the Vatican gardens

149 Michelangelo. Plan for San Giovanni de' Fiorentini, Rome. First design, 1559. Casa Buonarroti, Florence (121 A)

150 Michelangelo. Plan for San Giovanni de' Fiorentini, Rome. Second design, 1559. Casa Buonarroti, Florence (120 A v)

151 Michelangelo. Plan for San Giovanni de' Fiorentini, Rome. Third design, 1559. Casa Buonarroti, Florence (124 A r)

152 Plan of the Sforza Chapel, Santa Maria Maggiore, Rome, *c.* 1560. Bibliothèque Nationale, Paris

153 Sforza Chapel, Santa Maria Maggiore, Rome, interior view

154 Porta Pia, Rome, façade. Engraving by B. Faleti after Michelangelo's design, 1568

155 Michelangelo. *Crucifixion with the Virgin and St John*, *c.* 1550/55. Drawing, black chalk, retouched in white pigment and grey wash, 16⅜ × 11¼ (41·5 × 28·5). British Museum, London (W.81)
156 Michelangelo. *Crucifixion*, *c.* 1560. Drawing, black chalk, 10⅞ × 9¼ (27·5 × 23·5). Courtesy the Executors of the Estate of Count Antoine Seilern
157 Michelangelo. *Holy Family with Saints*, *c.* 1553. Cartoon, black chalk, 91¾ × 65⅜ (233 × 166). British Museum, London (W.75)
158 Michelangelo. *Annunciation*, *c.* 1560. Drawing, black chalk, 11⅛ × 7¾ (28 × 19·5). British Museum, London (W.72 r)
159 Michelangelo. *Pietà*, *c.* 1547–55. Marble, h. 89 (226). Florence Cathedral
160 Michelangelo. Sketches for the *Rondanini Pietà*, *c.* 1555. Black chalk, 4¼ × 11 (11 × 28). Ashmolean Museum, Oxford (P.339)
161 Michelangelo. *Rondanini Pietà*, 1555–64. Marble (unfinished), h. 76¾ (195). Castello Sforzesco, Milan

Photographic Acknowledgments

Colour

Scala 39, 47, 50, 55–6, 60–2, 66–7, 70–1, 74–5, 116–17, 132–3
Eileen Tweedy 40, 46

Black and white

Alinari 1–2, 6–7, 10–16, 26–7, 30–2, 36, 69, 81, 85–6, 90, 93, 95, 101, 103–4, 106–7, 113, 115, 129, 139, 140, 145, 153, 159, 161
Alinari-Anderson 21, 28, 38, 49, 51–4, 57–9, 63–5, 68, 72–3, 76–8, 97, 114, 118, 141, 146
Alinari-Brogi 17, 29, 34, 41, 88–9, 94, 109, 134
Civico Gabinetto Fotografico, Ferrara 18
Courtauld Institute of Art, London 42
Deutsches Archäologisches Institut, Rome 45
Gabinetto Fotografico Nazionale, Rome 136
Giraudon 4, 8, 20, 35, 83–4
Istituto Centrale per il Catalogo e la Documentazione, Rome 24, 87, 130–1
Leonard von Matt 96, 98–9, 137–8, 148
Réunions des Musées Nationaux, Paris 135
Soprintendenza alle Gallerie, Florence 108, 149–51

Index

Numbers in italics refer to illustrations